Will Hindus Develop and Secure India?

Will Hindus Develop and Secure India?

ATLURU SITARAMAIAH

VIKAS PUBLISHING HOUSE PVT LTD

VIKAS PUBLISHING HOUSE PVT LTD

576 Masjid Road, Jangpura, New Delhi-110 014
Phones: 4315313 4315570, 4314605 ☆ *Fax*: 4310879
e-mail: chawlap@giasdl01.vsnl.net.in ☆ *Internet*: www.ubspd.com

First Floor, N.S. Bhawan, 4th Cross 4th Main
Gandhi Nagar, Bangalore-560 009 ☆ Phone: 2204639

F-20, Nand Dham Industrial Estate, Marol,
Andheri (East), Mumbai-400 059 ☆ Phone: 8500461

Distributors:

UBS PUBLISHERS' DISTRIBUTORS LTD.

5 Ansari Road, New Delhi-110 002
Phones : 3273601, 3266646 ☆ *Cable* : ALLBOOKS ☆ *Fax* : 3276593, 3274261
e-mail: ubspd.del@smy.sprintrpg.ems.vsnl.net.in ☆ *Internet*: www.ubspd.com

10 First Main Road, Gandhi Nagar, Bangalore-560 009
Phones : 2263901, 2263902, 2253903 ☆ *Cable* : ALLBOOKS ☆ *Fax* : 2263904

6, Sivaganga Road, Nungambakkam, Chennai-600 034
Phone : 8276355 ☆ *Cable* : UBSIPUB ☆ *Fax* : 8270189

8/1-B, Chowringhee Lane, Calcutta-700 016
Phones : 2441821, 2442910, 2449473 ☆ *Cable* : UBSIPUBS ☆ *Fax* : 2450027

5 A, Rajendra Nagar, Patna-800 016
Phones : 672856, 656170 ☆ *Cable* : UBSPUB ☆ *Fax* : 656169

80, Noronha Road, Cantonment, Kanpur-208 004
Phones : 369124, 362665, 357488 ☆ *Fax* : 315122

Overseas Contact:

475 North Circular Road, Neasden, London NW2 7QG
Tele: 081-450-8667 ☆ *Fax*: 0181-452-6612 *Attn*: UBS

Distributors for Western India:

M/s Preface Books

Shivali Apartments, Plot No. 1, S. No. 25/4, Chintamani Society,
Karve Nagar, Pune 411052 ☆ *Phone*: 349491

First Published, 1999

Printed at Nutech Photolithographers, Delhi

Table of Contents

Acknowledgement

I wish to thank my wife Edda for her encouragement and support for this project. I am also grateful for her help in the preparation of the manuscript.

Introduction

India is an enigma to most peoples of the world. It is an old civilisation but in the contemporary world it remains backward and the outlook for it is bleak to mediocre at best. While the East Asian countries including China are on the verge of conquering and eliminating poverty from their societies, India continues to remain a symbol of poverty and filth. The country is irrelevant in international affairs and commerce. Any recognition accorded to it by the international community is due to size of its population rather than to any of its achievements. Its citizens and leaders, for the most part, are unable or unwilling to identify and implement the fundamental transformations the Indian society needs to undergo if it is to move forward confidently into the modern age. Undoubtedly, India has made some economic progress in the fifty years since its independence from British rule. But the basic value systems have hardly changed over the centuries and they remain rigid and least helpful for building a modern nation.

For example, an essential characteristic of developed and rapidly developing countries is that of work ethic. The vast majority of people in these societies believe in work, in its dignity and its importance to both material and spiritual well-being of the individual. In countries such as China and

South Korea men and women have strong work ethic and do not shy away from working hard for long hours. They respect work and consider it an important and essential aspect of life. Is it any wonder then that these countries have been able to achieve phenomenal rates of economic growth? Of course, the work ethic and dignity of work in the Western world is all too well known. However, in Indian society work, especially physical work is considered more or less demeaning and something to avoid if possible. This attitude is particularly prevalent among middle and rich classes of society. This lack of work ethic has, and will continue to have, an adverse impact on the country's productivity and quality of work.

The Indian day-to-day vocabulary is notably lacking in aphorisms on work such as "if you do something you might as well do it right" which have a significant impact on the attitude towards work. Adages such as "every human being has the right and an obligation to reach his or her full potential" are somewhat alien to Indian culture. Obviously, a society that embraces and believes in these values is better prepared to meet the challenges of building a modern and a dynamic nation. In the final analysis it is the citizens who build the country. When they reach their potential the society does as well. In progressive countries the governments and communities go at lengths to build infrastructures which facilitate citizens of all ages to develop and sharpen their talents, whatever they might be, which is an essential prerequisite to achieving their potential. Successive Indian governments, irrespective of their political affiliation, have been attempting to develop the country without much focus on the development of the individual. They are more interested, for example, in continuing to invest tax payers money in PSUs [public sector undertakings] even after the economy is opened to private investment than to take that money out and invest it to improve the quality of education and training for the poor. Somehow the Indian society has lost its direction and priorities. A society that treats individuals as unimportant has little chance of becoming a strong and progressive nation. A strong society is made up of strong individuals. Any society that ignores this is destined to remain weak or mediocre at best.

In a pluralistic society such as India where many different minority groups co-exist it is important that its political institutions protect these groups with utmost sensitivity and care if the country is to achieve maximum economic growth. Otherwise the society would waste its scarce resources and talents fighting each other resulting in reduced growth. As well, minority group members would not achieve their maximum potential if they are suppressed or restricted in anyway which in turn restricts the country from achieving its full potential. India does not have an acceptable record of protecting its minority groups. While the country professes to be a secular nation, it has been unable to successfully put this commitment into practice. The country cannot hope to achieve higher levels of growth with restless and unhappy minority groups. Only when every one of its citizens participates in building the country, can the country have the wherewithal to become a prosperous and dynamic nation.

Even in matters of defence the country suffers from a lack of appropriate value systems. After living under the Mogul and the British subjugation for one thousand years, one would expect the Indian people to be ever vigilant and be prepared to make whatever sacrifices necessary to defend their country and their freedoms. During the 1962 border war, the Chinese army walked right across the Indian border with impunity and India was helpless and unable to stop the incursion. The Chinese army was able to do whatever it wished. India and its people were put to shame and disgraced. Even today, if they wish to do so, the Chinese army could walk right through India again with little, if any, resistance from the Indian army. They could move from the Himalayas to the southern tip of India with such lightening speed that the Indians wouldn't know what hit them. What is holding the Chinese back is their own strategy and calculations, certainly not the fear of the Indian army. Yet Indians have been mostly oblivious to the Chinese threat until the defence minister George Fernandes first brought it to their attention in early 1998. It escaped their imagination for too long. Why? Their value systems prevented them from grasping the seriousness of the threat to their freedom and the high price they have to pay to defend it. Despite its long history of subjugation, the Indian society is still incapable of understanding the preciousness of freedom, the constant vigilance, and high degree of alertness and military preparedness required in order to ensure its freedoms and security of its territory.

India exploded its first nuclear device in 1974 and five more in 1998, test fired long range missiles, more recently developed high speed advanced computers and yet it remains militarily weak and still has no effective defences against China. Worst still is that it cannot focus on this issue and engages in wishful thinking, that China can be appeased by minimizing the significance of the border dispute with it. Meanwhile the Chinese troops make regular forays inside Indian territory. They have also commissioned nuclear weapons and missiles aimed at India in Tibet. Indian politicians simply do not know how to react to all these moves beyond conducting some nuclear tests and therefore they talk gibberish which no one can understand. The worst of all is that Indian people put up with this nonsense.

The country seems to have the resources and abilities to transform itself into a modern and progressive nation and yet it lacks the resolve, commitment and sense of purpose. The distinguished news magazine, *The Economist*, aptly puts this in perspective. In its January 3rd, 1998 edition it says India "always seems to be held back by something." As mentioned earlier, it exploded a nuclear device in 1974 but was afraid to produce and induct nuclear weapons immediately following the test. Instead it waited for Pakistan to catch up. Test fired long range missiles but chose not to produce them in quantity for defence, again waited, until Pakistan caught up with it. Developed high speed computers but has not put marketing muscle behind them to sell them worldwide in any significant way. It introduced economic reforms but has been reluctant to divest non-defence related PSUs and so on. The country displays a pathological inability to take matters to their logical conclusion. It takes one step forward and two steps back. It would appear that Indians abhor success and back away from it when they get close to it.

Politicians seem more focused on slogans and ideologies than doing whatever is necessary for building the country. They are more bent on exploiting the worst instincts of people such as caste and religious hatreds than on appealing to their best talents for developing the country. It does not seem to bother them that the country is falling behind many of the Asian countries. They do not seem to understand the real connection between economic prosperity, and social justice and national security.

Building and securing India is a monumental task which requires clear thinking, focus, unwavering commitment, unparalleled mobilisation of resources, strengthening of individual, strong work ethic and so on. Does the Indian society have the necessary values and character to measure up to the task?

This book explores the current value systems of the society and how they correlate against the values necessary for building and securing a modern and progressive India.

Chapter 1

Hindu Values

Indian society is predominantly Hindu and hence its culture and values dominate the society. Although there are several significant minority groups which play a vital role in every aspect of the society, dominance of Hindus is a fact of life. Muslims are the largest of these minority groups. Following the partition of India, they are uncertain of their role in the predominantly Hindu society. When they sort out their thinking, feel secure and begin to fully participate in building the nation they can make a considerable difference for the better.

Basically when we talk about the values of today's Indian society we are primarily referring to the Hindus Values. It is not that the values of the other groups are not important but their influence is more regional. For example, the Sikh influence in Punjab and New Delhi is undeniably a large factor. But at the national level, the cultural and political dominance of Hindus is indisputable. The future of India rests largely upon their shoulders, at least in the foreseeable future. They have to take the blame should India fail to measure up to its potential. The converse would be true as well. We must understand the psyche and value systems of

Hindus if we are to make a judgment as to what the future holds for India. These values are mostly the result of their past one thousand years of history and of course their religion.

A very brief review of Hindu experiences during their subjugation period is essential to understanding its impact on Hindu character and behaviour. Then the probable values that they developed as a result of these experiences can be identified.

Impact of Subjugation on Hindu Values

The Mogul conquest of India changed Hindu character and values so deeply that they are still well entrenched and continue to shape their thinking and behaviour. The conquest began with Mahmud Gazni in the year 997 A.D. which might be considered the beginning of subjugation of Hindus by foreign conquerors. This was not a sudden or unexpected event. By the time he arrived at the Indian borders the Hindu society had begun to disintegrate because of internal divisions and jealousies, and further it had become disinterested in shouldering responsibilities for national security and defence. Will Durant in his series *The Story of Civilisation* observed "the Hindus had allowed their strengths to be wasted in internal division and war; they had adopted religions like Buddhism and Jainism, which unnerved them for the tasks of life; that they had failed to organize their forces for the protection of their frontiers and their Capitals, their wealth and their freedom, from the hordes of Scythians, Huns, Afgans and Turks hovering about India's boundaries and waiting for national weakness to let them in. For four hundred years [600-1000 A.D] India invited conquest and at last it came."

The Mogul conquerors despised the Hindu religion and its offshoots, and their followers. They spared no effort in slaughtering them by hundreds of thousands and destroyed everything they valued and owned. Their temples were pillaged and burned. The civilians and their leaders were murdered for no other reason than that they were Hindus. Will Durant noted in the book referred to earlier that "Sultan Ahmed feasted for three days whenever the number of defenceless Hindus slain in his territories in one day reached twenty thousand." There were numerous examples of senseless cruelty and brutality throughout the history of Mogul rule. Hindus became near-slaves in their own country, were reduced to poverty, and forced to live under appalling conditions of filth and terror. This was very similar to European colonisation, terrorisation, and genocidal killings of the indigenous population in the Americas. Hindus did very little to overturn the Mogul rule. They took refuge in their religion and accepted whatever indignities and insults Moguls threw at them

By the time the European [British] conquerors arrived Hindus could not have been in any worse condition than they were. They were dispossessed, dispirited, demoralised, and disinterested.

The European conquest of India began with the Portuguese around 1510 A.D. and concluded with the English about 1760 A.D. The English rule was not any better than the Mogul rule. They also pillaged and further impoverished the nation. Like the Moguls, they treated natives as near-slaves. The principal difference between the Mogul and the British rule was that the English did not commit wholesale slaughter of Hindus. They were happy with plundering the country and forcing Hindus to live in poverty and near starvation.

The foregoing should give enough of a flavour of the conditions in which Hindus lived for almost one thousand years [in the interest of accuracy it should be pointed out that different regions of India lived under the Mogul rule for different lengths of time since it took time to extend their rule across the country] until the year 1947, the year of independence. They lived in constant fear for their life and limb, their properties and possessions confiscated for no reason, all the while being forced to live like slaves in near starvation conditions. Famines were very common. For nearly one thousand years they were at the lowest end of the political and social structure, utterly despised, with very little or no hope for improvement in their appalling living conditions. Most of them lived in filth and squalor. No other race in the world was subjugated for as long as the Hindus were. What was particularly sad about Hindus was that they vastly outnumbered both the Moguls and the English who conquered and ruled them, yet they were unable to overthrow them and their rule. They had taken an incredibly long time to free themselves. Whether Hindus admit it or not, their religion was an unwitting ally of Mogul and English rulers. They knew it and some rulers like Akbar used it to their advantage. It helped them control the Hindu masses and provided irrational rationale and a philosophical basis for Hindus to accept their condition regardless of how bad and horrible it was.

The purpose of the foregoing discussion is not to judge the history, but to make use of it to identify the characteristics that Hindus acquired from these historical experiences. Any sociologist would likely conclude that the Mogul and the British subjugation would change the Hindu character and values to embrace the following:

Lack of Respect for Law and Order

This is to be expected because Mogul and English laws were designed to dispossess, oppress and repress Hindus. So they grew up with no respect for law and order. Why wouldn't they? This lack of respect for law was so well ingrained and it continues to persist in the present day India. Very few Hindus believe in the supremacy of the law. There is only a shallow commitment to it and every one including politicians would do anything to get around it. Some take law into their hands and go unpunished for their crimes. Criminals get elected to the legislative bodies. Yet it does not bother the conscience of the vast majority of Hindus.

In fact most Hindus do not understand the importance and role of law in ensuring order in a democratic society. Even many leaders of the country do not consider the law of the land as supreme and to be that which needs to be upheld under any circumstances. For example, on February 21, 1998 the governor of the province of Utter Pradesh dismissed the then BJP government in power because he thought it lacked a majority support in the Provincial Assembly. It is not our purpose to discuss the relative merits of this decision. A.B.Vajpayee, the then prime ministerial candidate of the BJP party announced immediately that he was going to go on a fast unto death unless the dismissal was reversed and the dismissed BJP government reinstated. This clearly has shown the lack of respect for law and order on the part of Mr. Vajpayee because he should have known that it was up to the courts to decide whether the governor had acted improperly. Instead he threatened to go on a fast unto death implying that any court decision should conform to his views otherwise he would kill himself. This was clearly anarchy and showed his clear disregard for the law of the land, whether he meant it or not. Is this any way for a prime ministerial candidate to promote respect for law in the society?

The idea of fast unto death was popularised by Mahatma Gandhi. He fasted because he wanted to defy the British rule in India and refused to respect their colonial laws. In the India of today the laws are enacted by the parliament of India, duly elected by the Indian people in free elections. Therefore, it is the sacred duty of Mr. Vajpayee, and every citizen of India, to respect the law of the land and promote adherence to it under any and all circumstances. Whenever a citizen feels that he has been wronged it is his duty to go to court seeking justice. But to go on a fast unto death is to take the court system for ransom which is equivalent to the complete breakdown of law and order.

The above example clearly shows lack of understanding, respect, and regard for law and order even among the top leadership of the country. Then how can an average person have any faith and respect for the law of the land?

Lack of Self-Confidence

Self-confidence and self-respect are gained by individuals or societies when they have achieved unparalleled accomplishments. These may include the building of monuments such as the Taj Mahal, the Great Wall of China, or discovering revolutionary theories such as the Theory of Relativity, or being the first to land a man on Mars, or building a very prosperous and powerful nation and so on. Self-confidence engenders a belief in individuals and societies that they are as competent as any and that they can compete with the best. It feeds on to itself as they accumulate more and more achievements to their credit

Nothing of great significance was achieved by Hindus in the past 1000 to 1500 years. They cannot take credit for the Taj Mahal. It was the accomplishment of the Moguls. Whatever accomplishments Hindus might have achieved were very modest by international standards. As a result their self-confidence level is low. Some Hindus might disagree with this. However, one cannot imagine that any society which was subjugated for as long as the Hindu society to possess a great deal of self-confidence. Since independence, the accomplishments of Hindus have been few and far between, if any, and did very little to build their self-confidence. There is no easy way to build self-confidence other than by major accomplishments in such fields as economy, science, engineering, architecture, military, medicine, sports and so on.

Less Accomplishment Oriented

Hindus were almost an enslaved race during their years of occupation. They had little desire or opportunity to accomplish anything of significance because they lacked resources and support from their masters. There was no way their rulers would encourage them to accomplish anything worthwhile. On the contrary they had done everything possible to put Hindus down and they succeeded for a very long time. Given these conditions, it has become a well ingrained habit for Hindus not to seek to be accomplishment oriented. This habit is still strong although to a lesser degree. Their desire for accomplishment weakens particularly when faced with intense competitive activity. Lack of self-confidence may also have something to do with it. Hindus' performance in most international sports and commerce for example is dismal. Even in areas where competition is not a major factor, such as major research projects, their accomplishments tend to be weak. One cannot conceive of Hindus being able to build something the magnitude of Great Wall of China. They may be able to start a project of that nature but they will more than likely have difficulty completing it. They lack stamina, concentration, a focus to stick with activities that either have a lot of competitive pressures and/or take a long time to execute.

Accomplishment orientation requires self-confidence, a strong desire to succeed, intense focus, and ability to plan every detail to execute flawlessly. Equally important, is the belief that they can do it.

Lost Ability to Govern

The most obvious consequence of subjugation is that almost all decision making power in the subjugated society moves to the subjugators. All the affairs of the society [i.e. finance, taxes, defence, security, police, education, health, public welfare, agriculture, industry, highways and transportation etc.] would be tightly controlled by them. The subjugated will have very little or no say in these matters. This is especially true when the subjugators' objective is to plunder and destroy the subjugated country. This was exactly what happened in the case of India. All decision making was controlled by the Moguls and the British during their respective rules. Hindus were not part of it although close to the end of British rule, some limited self-rule was allowed in certain areas. However, the important state matters such as finance, taxes, defence, security etc. were always tightly controlled by the Moguls and the British. Hindus were denied all exposure to governing during the foreign rule. Consequently, they lost whatever governing skills they had prior to the Mogul period and this is clearly evident in India today. Many Indian politicians today do not have the skills for effective governance and are woefully inadequate for the job. Most of them are like kids in a candy store. They believe they can get away with anything and therefore abuse power believing it is there to help themselves and their families. Their understanding of finance, defence, security, economic development, international relations and so on is shallow and naïve, if not farcical at times. For example they do not see grave dangers to nation's financial health and security when governments run up huge fiscal deficits. Another example was the venomous comments made by the Home Minister Mr. L.K.Advani and some of the Prime Minister Vajpayee's advisors threatening Pakistan immediatly following India's nuclear tests in May 1998. They were a clear illustration of immaturity and lack of experience in governing.

Vast majority of politicians are ill equipped to communicate complex issues with the masses and mobilise them to any significant degree to achieve critical national objectives. As a result the elite and bureaucrats have taken control of the government and have a stranglehold on power.

Sadly, the society lacks role models from its recent past in leadership who displayed extraordinary abilities in governing the country during critical periods of national life. As a result, the society feels hopeless, at times, because it does not know really what to look for in a leader. The society has not experienced good governing for nearly 1200 to 1500 years and thus lacks standards for anyone to aspire to. It does not look like that it is going to have anyone soon, either.

Acceptance of Filth and Squalor in Daily Life

There is no society in the world that tolerates and accepts filth and squalor among their midst as does the Hindu society. When they were under foreign domination the rulers forced Hindus into poverty by confiscating their property and possessions, while forcing them to live in squalor. The rulers were not prepared to spend money to improve sanitary conditions in places where Hindus resided. This resulted in Hindus accepting the ugliness and unsanitary conditions in their midst as part of their landscape. They became desensitised and hence no longer offended by it. The habit has become well ingrained and there are no signs they want to or can change. If cleanliness is indeed next to Godliness, then, Hindus have to be the worst offenders of Godliness.

Hindus' insensitivity to filth and squalor defies imagination and offends human decency. Today they are masters of their own house and should be able to change it if they want to. Obviously they do not want to, or do not care, or do not recognise it as a problem. Living in this manner not only degrades the environment, it also breeds deadly diseases of various kinds, and more importantly degrades human spirit and destroys human dignity. Any civilised country would have initiated a national campaign to get rid of the filth and clean up the country as soon as it became independent. But Hindus do not seem to be bothered by it in the least.

Distrust of Foreign Powers and Foreign Multinational Corporations

Given the long history of subjugation, it is understandable that Hindus do not trust foreign powers and multinational corporations. Naturally they do not want their history repeated. While it is desirable to always keep an eye on foreign powers and their machinations, it is not helpful or useful to become paranoid about it. If the objective is to protect themselves from history ever repeating itself then it is more logical and useful to constantly interact with foreign powers to better understand them and their values and become good at playing their game.

Western powers believe that their citizens have the right to a good life and that the earth and its resources are for the enjoyment of human beings. They believe that they have an obligation and a right to shape the world in a way consistent with their values, beliefs and interests. The powers act in their best self interest and expect every country to do the same. They despise and pity the weak and the poor and have no use whatsoever for those who moralize everything yet do very little to improve themselves or fight for their self interest. Western countries firmly believe that the future belongs to those who have an edge on technology, trade and commerce and military strength. Hindus can only protect themselves by understanding this and by developing and successfully executing appropriate strategies in response to it. They cannot protect themselves by withdrawing from foreign powers or by building a fortress around themselves.

The Hindus' fear of multinationals is irrational. India receives billions of dollars in foreign aid and loans, yet they see no danger or shame in it but they see danger in allowing multinationals to operate in their country. They fail to recognise that borrowing money from foreign countries is far more threatening to their freedoms than allowing multinationals to operate in their country. The latter not only have an obligation but also can be legally forced to follow and respect domestic laws, whereas aid donors have a right to tell the borrowers how to run their economy, social policy, defence, and even what kind of political system is appropriate for them. This is one of the principal differences between China and India. China does not depend upon foreign aid and therefore foreign powers do not have any leverage on it; whereas India depends on aid and therefore the donor countries can and do exercise control on it. The economic sanctions following India's nuclear tests in May 1998 is a clear example of this.

It is demeaning to continue to depend on foreign aid even after fifty years of independence. Depending on multinationals is much more preferable, every country does it including developed countries and they can be buttressed to help build the economy faster and without any threat to national security.

Low Self-Esteem and Self-Respect

The Moguls and the British hated Hindus and their way of life and forced them to live under disrespectful and demeaning conditions for nearly one thousand years. Under such circumstances it was very difficult, if not impossible, to expect Hindu children to grow up developing much self-esteem and self-respect. They hardly had good real life role models to pattern their aspirations. They could see their parents and their community humbling before the Moguls and the British and doing very little to get rid of the yoke of foreign oppression and domination. It was hardly the environment for a child to develop self-respect and self-esteem.

Very Little Compassion and Respect for Fellow Citizens

The colonial masters [the Moguls and the British] despised Hindus and showed no compassion or mercy towards them. Neither did they value the life of Hindus. They slaughtered them by the thousands with impunity and mistreated them in every way imaginable. Hindus learned the same from their masters and learned it well. Today Hindus have very little compassion and respect for their fellow citizens. They hate lower caste people and trample on their rights. It is not uncommon for some Hindus to take the law into their own hands, like their colonial masters did, and butcher and maim fellow citizens simply because of their caste or religion. People in power behave in the same manner as their colonial masters did. They feel superior to the people they are supposed to be serving. People hardly treat a fellow citizen with graciousness and respect unless the person is related or wealthy or powerful.

The foregoing describes a very significant part of the psyche of Hindus which they acquired during the Mogul and the British rule. Much more than what is presented above can supplement the theme but our focus is on identifying only what is relevant for our purpose.

Impact of Religion on Hindu Values

To complete the picture of the Hindu psyche, we should now turn our attention to the impact the Hindu religion has on the psyche especially as it relates to economic development, social relations, and national security. The purpose is not to evaluate or judge Hinduism but to identify the relevant characteristics it helped shape on its followers. We are not interested in what is written in the Hindu scriptures but our focus is on identifying the actual characteristics which can be found in a vast majority of Hindus in their daily life. In other words our objective is to identify actual characteristics rather than what should be or what should have been according to the scriptures. These are:

A vast majority of Hindus have never been exposed to clearly identified and documented values in a formal setting to guide their day-to-day lives in a practical manner.

Hindus, adults and children alike, learn their values mainly from their own personal experiences and interactions with the fellow citizens. They rarely receive instructions in a formal setting from a learned person in an organised way. Parents and school teachers play a limited role in imparting values to children usually in a casual setting. But for the most part children do not get full exposure to the values necessary even for good learning, let alone values to guide them through life. The Hindu religion is not an organised religion unlike Christianity, Judaism, Islam, Sikhism, and Buddhism and so on. These religions, unlike Hinduism require their followers to get together at their places of worship at least once a week at which time the minister [priest] not only conducts religious prayers but also lectures and discusses the fundamental values necessary, such as work ethic, to lead a rewarding life and also contribute to building a better society. In many cases these weekly gatherings afford an opportunity for individuals to recharge, rejuvenate and reinvigorate their commitment to basic values necessary to be productive and descent citizens. Unfortunately, Hindus do not have similar gatherings. Theirs are for religious prayers but never to present, discuss and promote those values which are necessary to help build a productive and caring society. This is perhaps one of the most glaring deficiencies of Hindu way of life.

There are some mythological religious stories passed on from one generation to another which are supposed to impart certain values but the effectiveness of such an approach under the best of circumstances is questionable. It may help a child who is fortunate enough to have educated and talented parents who can explain the stories but most children are denied such privilege.

As a result there are no firm anchors in Hindu character and it shifts like desert sand.

Hindus lach community spirit and community values

This is one of the major weaknesses of Hindu society. They lack love and commitment to the community in which they live. As mentioned earlier, most religions are organised at least at a community level. Followers belong to a local Gurudwara, or Mosque, or Buddhist temple or Church whatever the individual case may be. Sometimes these local institutions are a part of a district-wide and/or province-wide organisation which in turn may be part of a nation-wide and/ or worldwide organisation. Usually there is a temporal head at the top providing direction, guidance and inspiration to the followers.

The head of the local institution provides moral guidance and values, exhorts followers to conduct themselves in an ethical manner consistent with their basic beliefs and values. Also, these institutions promote fraternal and community spirit and inculcate values necessary to build a strong, vibrant, and caring community.

Hindus do not have such local institutions which help contribute to the development of community spirit and community values. These institutions should not be confused with local temples which are mainly for worship. The temple priest never addresses the temple audience and rarely, if ever, gets involved in the development of community spirit and values. Basically Hindus are left to their own devices to develop values suitable for themselves, their family and their communities unlike Sikhs, Muslims, Christians, Buddhists etc.

As a result, over the years there has been a degeneration of Hindu character. It has become corrupt, unreliable, and lacking in community spirit, and sense of justice. In the best of times human beings need outside pressure to remind them to stick to basic values and community obligations. When there is no such pressure, the character of the community is bound to deteriorate and degenerate. Is it any wonder then why there is so much corruption and lack of community spirit in India?

Hindus lack discipline to succeed in highly competitive and /or high risk environment.

Hindus are as intelligent as any people in the world but they lack discipline to succeed in activities and situations such as sports, military and paramilitary activities and the like, international disputes with high stakes attached to them, and highly competitive international business environments and so on. Why is this so?

Webster's dictionary defines discipline as "training which corrects, moulds, strengthens or perfects". To improve one's chances of success consistently one needs discipline, meaning one improves performance by identifying and correcting his weaknesses, and practices the improved version until it becomes second nature. The process of improvement and practice goes on until the person feels confident that he/she can do better than the opponent and therefore it engenders self-confidence as well. Acquiring a disciplined approach to things is a complex task to say the least and can be best learned in formal settings. Only organisations are best equipped to impart discipline because they usually have resources, motivation, and expertise. For example, military organisations, boy and girl scout clubs, sports clubs, flying clubs, dance clubs, swimming clubs are some organisations which impart discipline. An interesting point with discipline is that if an individual who went through the discipline routine once to become an expert at a certain activity [e.g. flying an airplane] he/she will have little difficulty in duplicating the routine to learn other activities.

A vast majority of Hindus get no exposure at all to any type of organisation other than school during their upbringing. Very few schools have resources, or the expertise, to impart rigorous discipline in any activity. Earlier it was pointed out that their religion is not organised at a community level. So, it plays no role in imparting discipline to the followers unlike some highly organised religions. Because of this lack of exposure to any organisation other than school in the early upbringing they are deprived of focus and intensity which only an organisation can teach, which makes most Hindus unsuitable and unreliable for tasks requiring these attributes such as fighting protracted wars, piloting airplanes, sports, international confrontations involving high stakes and so on.

Other advantages of belonging or associating with an organisation in early stages of upbringing, in addition to learning discipline, are that an individual learns the importance of co-operation, fairness, integrity, and team spirit which are weak in Hindu character. An example of this is the shameful and disgusting treatment meted out to the Suzuki Motor Corporation by the Indian government. Anyone with integrity and a sense of fair play would never treat an equal partner which helped India build a respectable automobile industry the way the Indian Government has done. In reality the partnership is not equal when one takes into account the fact that the Indian Government is a sovereign power whereas Suzuki Motor Corporation has no power except for the power to withdraw from the partnership or engage in a legal battle in an international court which costs money and time. This puts extra onus on the Government to be extremely fair in its dealings. But it lacks the discipline to be so.

This lack of discipline in Hindu character mostly explains why the world is reluctant to recognise India as one of the world leaders. The world finds very little inspiring or reassuring in Hindu character.

Values Intellectual Pursuits more than Physical Pursuits

This has a lot to do with Hindu religious philosophy which values life after death more than life here and now. Life here and now is mostly physical and practical, whereas life after death is theoretical and intellectualised. For most Hindus, life here is meaningless and not important. Then it follows that achievements here and now have little value. By deprecating life here they are, in turn, placing little value on physical pursuits of life which make life here enjoyable and exciting. But material well-being is essential to happiness in daily life which cannot be attained without vigorous pursuit. Therefore Hindus are torn with this dilemma. They cannot pursue material well-being in this life with full conviction. Quite often they are blase about it. This is one of the reasons why they are not offended as much by the grinding poverty in their midst. It does not bother them that they are left behind while most of the rest of Asia is moving far ahead of them in eliminating poverty and thus making life more enjoyable for their citizens. They simply have this smug feeling that they know better.

In reality, most Hindus love the material aspects of life but are afraid to admit it openly. As a result, for example, the society is hesitant to intensify its efforts for building materially abundant society with singular focus, or to engage in the creation of beautiful monuments such as the Eiffel tower, the Taj Mahal etc. because the contradiction between such material achievements and their beliefs would be blatantly apparent to everyone in the world and to themselves.

Of course, the positive side of valuing intellectual pursuits is that Hindus are good in such things as mathematics, computer software, chess etc. but, poor in anything requiring physical discipline such as sports, design and production of things that make physical aspects of life more enjoyable and so on.

As noted earlier Hindus value life after death, more so than life here and now and therefore they have put themselves in the position of having to intellectualise everything because as observed earlier life after death is theoretical, speculative and can be visualised only intellectually. That leads to the habit of excessive rhetoric, moralisation, and generalisation. For this reason Hindu intellectuals can talk in circles endlessly while justifying everything and anything, as long as it does not involve action and responsibility. Their thinking is far removed from the realities of life. That is the main reason why Hindus are not considered to be practical people. For example, it is not in their character to say "that is enough talking, let us go and do something useful." There is absolutely nothing wrong being intellectually powerful but it is a grave deficiency not to be practical. Undoubtedly, this lack of practicality contributed considerably why Hindus had taken so long to free themselves from the foreign rule, for example.

Hindus cannot mount a difficult sustained campaign over a long period to achieve important national goals

This is mainly because almost all national campaigns such as building an economy, fighting a war are materialistic in nature, in the sense they are related in one form or another making life on earth enjoyable and secure on which Hindu religion puts very little emphasis. Many Hindus wouldn't care to give singular focus to such activities.

Mounting a sustained campaign requires an unwavering and unshakable commitment to objectives and goals, extraordinary motivation, self-confidence, discipline, practicality, and action. An overwhelming majority of Hindus do not seem to have an unwavering commitment to anything, especially in situations when the odds are against them. The last time they displayed it was when they were fighting the British for independence. That was a very rare event in Indian history in which all minority groups took part and played a major role, and also the British were not ready to fight to stay in India at any cost. But it is only a remote probability, if not impossibility that a commitment of that nature could ever be mustered again. The reason being the major issues facing them today are economic, national security, and social justice for which Hindus cannot get too enthused. Economic issues are too materialistic for Hindus to give an unwavering commitment, as mentioned earlier; social justice is something they cannot get too excited about due to caste and religious bigotry; and when it comes to national security they cannot imagine ever engaging in a protracted war, if they need to, with a country like China and winning. They lack discipline to buckle up and get to work, stay focused and give everything they have to solve the problems.

In addition, Hindus simply avoid situations where the emphasis is only on action and where there is no room for rhetoric. This is a major reason why they love to belong to organisations such as the Non-Aligned Movement and G-15 because the stock in trade of these organisations is rhetoric and moralisation and is completely devoid of any action and responsibility.

Pathological Antipathy to Success, at Society Level

Success in our context implies realisation of a goal or an objective which contributes to improving well-being of a society. It is materialistic in the sense it contributes to bettering life on earth. Most of society's goals and objectives take a long time, sometimes inordinately long to fully realise, which means they demand a lot of discipline, stamina and concentration to stay focused. In addition success is determined by the degree of ambition, motivation, commitment, and of course the level of effort. Technical factors such as quality of plans and execution will have a bearing as well.

Hindus for the most part shun public admission of ambition. For example, politicians do not publicly admit that they aspire to become a chief minister or a prime minister even when it is their intent. They are afraid to discuss, during their political campaigns why they feel they are better qualified for the job than their opponent. One is expected to show his or her ambition indirectly and discreetly. That may work for an individual, but how could a society be discreet or indirect in expressing its collective goals and ambitions? How would it be possible to set ambitious goals for a society without looking to be ambitious? Yet ambition is the foundation of success, and without it there will be very little commitment, motivation and will to succeed. Therefore it is very difficult to set ambitious goals for Hindu society which can enjoy wide support, especially if the risks are high.

It was noted earlier that Hindus have difficulty to stay focused over a long period of time to achieve important national goals and objectives which are always materialistic in nature. Usually most execution plans to achieve them are implemented in stages. Since Hindus cannot maintain focus for as long as many of these plans require, as soon as some of the initial benefits are realised the leaders will do something deliberately to divert the attention of the public away from the plans, so to speak to give them a break, and also to satisfy opponents of the objectives. There will be little outcry against it from the public because they cannot and do not want to maintain focus on the objectives for as long as required anyway. For example, this is the reason whenever it looks as though India is making good progress in reforming and restructuring its economy, they [the bureaucrats and/or the ministers] do something or other without fail to jeopardize it. You can almost predict it and can count on it. This behaviour is consistent with the other Hindu belief that the human being is not in charge of his/her destiny but that fate dictates everything. So, they take solace by believing that fate really did not intend full realisation of the objectives. In the end very few get upset or unhappy for not fully realising the objectives. Many would say success is not really that important! This kind twisted logic is behind why Hindu society displays such a pathological antipathy to success.

Hindus Lack Respect forHuman Rights

Hindu society has been based on a caste system for centuries and it is essentially the same today. This aspect of the society has hardly changed over time. The system has assigned certain duties and responsibilities to certain castes and has ensured their enforcement through social pressures and coercion.

Beyond those duties and responsibilities assigned by the caste system there have been no discernible fundamental rights applicable to all regardless of the caste. Importantly, there was never any recognition, in practice, by Hindus of the fundamental equality of human beings, irrespective of what was in Hindu scriptures or the Indian constitution. Very few Hindus believe in it, even today. The fundamental basis for human rights is human equality. A society that does not believe in human equality cannot claim that it believes in human rights.

Mahatma Gandhi tried to convince the Hindus of the evils of caste system and tried to impress upon them the fundamental equality of human being but he failed. His efforts made very little difference. The beliefs are so well entrenched in the society, it is doubtful if they will ever accept equality of citizens regardless of their caste or religion. Without a thought or discussion lower caste citizens' rights are routinely subordinated for the so called overall good of the society which is usually decided by a small group of elitists in power. The Hindu establishment turns a blind eye to these injustices. For example, following the Pokhran nuclear tests in May 1998 some nearby villagers complained about the damage to their health and property as a result of the tests. Very little attention was paid to their pleas for adequate compensation and medical care. All in the name of greater good of the society.

The Hindu society is one among those in the world which are least sensitive to human rights.

Hindus do not have National Security Orientation

Hindu religion has been more inward than outward looking, at least in the past 1500 years. Subjects such as territorial integrity, defence, international politics, exploring foreign countries and their cultures has had very little attraction to Hindu mind. These were thrust upon Hindus since the European conquest of India. Several Chinese scholars visited ancient India to explore Indian culture and had written about it. But very few, if any Indian scholars visited ancient China to learn about their culture. Today if one were interested in learning about the history of ancient India the only sources of first hand accounts are the writings of Greek and Chinese visitors during that period. Outsiders knew more about India than Hindus did of them.

If a society is not inquisitive about its neighbours, to learn and understand their culture and their way of life, that would mean that the society does not care about potential security threats from them or simply does not understand national security or both. This was exactly what happened in the case of India. Hindus had shown very little curiosity or interest in learning about their neighbours prior to or during the Mogul and English rule because matters of national security never captured their imagination. To a lesser extent the attitude still persists to this day. Very few Hindus show interest in national security matters beyond shouting slogans. This includes their attitude towards fighting. Very few believe that it is their duty to fight for the country, if necessary, to defend its borders and freedoms. However, it should be pointed out that many Hindus would want to fight Pakistan, if required, because of religious hatred. But that is not the same as objectively accepting the obligation to fight for the country no matter who the enemy might be. For example, very few Hindus would offer to fight China because a vast majority of Hindus are motivated by religious hatred than by national duty to fight for the country. In addition they are scared of China because it is stronger.

The values identified in this chapter largely shaped the character and behaviour of Hindus and their society and how they respond to various situations, problems and challenges facing them. These values control the amount of energy, effort, motivation, and dedication that they are willing to put into understanding, solving and coping with problems and challenges facing the country.

Chapter 2

Development Value Systems

We have reviewed thus far some of the basic value systems of Hindu culture pertinent to economic and social development, and national security. Some of these have been inherent to the culture itself and some were acquired during the Mogul and the British rule. We have not delved into the Hindu Scriptures because our interest is in identifying what is prevalent in practice rather than what should be or should have been. If a value recommended in Scriptures is not practised in real life then one has to conclude that that particular value has no bearing on the society. For example, Christianity teaches that if a person is slapped on one of his cheeks then he should turn the other check as well. No one does that in the Western world. That particular religious preaching is irrelevant if one wants to understand people living in that part of the world. It is very rare that people follow every religious teaching because realities of life make it difficult to do so. This is true with all religions.

We will now turn our focus to identifying value systems critical to achieving rapid economic and social growth and to ensuring national security by observing the experiences of some successful societies. We will then analyse the suitability of Hindu values for achieving the same. Hopefully, it will point out what changes are necessary in the value systems of Hindus for them to be able to successfully develop India into an economic powerhouse and ensure its security.

If a country is to achieve a balanced growth it will have to focus on four areas:

1. Economic,
2. Social,
3. Political, and
4. National security.

Some countries fail to achieve balanced growth because they focus mainly in one or two of the four areas and accomplish phenomenal growth in those areas, but the lack of balance creates social tensions and cracks in these societies which can sometimes lead to social unrest. China is a classical example. It is attempting to develop its society by focusing only in three of the four areas, the economic, social and national security aspects. But it continues to deny progress in the political arena. Freedoms of its people remain repressed. Eventually, this can lead to social unrest in the country. Therefore balanced growth is essential to a stable and secure society. But balanced growth does not imply slower growth. It simply implies that if one or two areas are given greater priority and emphasis then the remaining should receive at least sufficient attention in order to ensure social peace and harmony.

The objective of this book is not to present a set of blueprints of specific objectives, programmes and plans for achieving a balanced and rapid growth. Although they are important by themselves, the focus in this book will be restricted to identifying the factors which determine the extent of abilities of a society in setting for itself challenging objectives and achieving them.

Ultimately it is the responsibility of the citizens and their leaders to build society. Their focus, motivation, and commitment to do so is governed by their fundamental value systems which determine the success or failure, slow or rapid, balanced or uneven growth. The focus here is to identify these fundamental value systems. This aspect of development has been ignored in post-independent India. The responsibility for developing the country was primarily assigned to the Central Government and its bureaucrats because the founder of modern India, Jawaharlal Nehru believed more in its abilities than in the abilities of an average citizen or even local governments to do the job effectively. This bias continues to persist to this day.

Over the 50 years since independence very few initiatives have been taken to strengthen the individual or local governments. For example, the Central Government felt it was more important to invest in such projects as huge steel plants than it was to invest in eradicating illiteracy and teaching people basic skills needed to qualify for a job. Most national leaders have always believed that the Central Government knows everything and that it has a better understanding for the citizens' requirements and their priorities than the citizens themselves, and also for what each and every province requires than the respective provincial governments themselves. These beliefs continue to be the underlying philosophy of governance which has contributed to the weakening of the individual.

Basically what has happened in the past 50 years was that the Central Government has strengthened itself at the expense of the individual and this continues even to this day. The basic needs of the average citizen have been shunted to the sidelines while the government has acquired more and more power over him in order to pursue its grandiose plans and ideologies. The individual has never been the center-piece of its plans. His needs and priorities have been subjugated to the use of scarce resources for the Central Government's ownership of industry. This must be reversed if the country is to be developed on a sound footing. The government should focus more on investing in ensuring that all citizens, including the poor, have the development values and skills and thus make it possible for them to active and leading roles in building the country than on investing in government ownership of industry. Strong countries are the result of strong citizens. In this respect India would be well off emulating China, Taiwan, and South Korea which have done an admirable job of educating and training their people.

A society must adopt appropriate development values in economic, social, and political spheres if it is to achieve rapid and balanced growth. It must treat individual as the primary instrument of change rather than the government and its bureaucrats. Dependence on individuals for change strengthens the society whereas dependence on bureaucrats strengthens only the government.

In the subsequent chapters a set of values are presented which, if adopted by a majority in the Hindu society, would not only strengthen the society but also give a tremendous boost to economic, social, political and military development of India.

Chapter 3

Economic Values

There are four fundamental values, pertaining to economic development, noticeable in the conduct and beliefs of citizens of the economic super powers: the U.S.A, Japan, and Germany. These have contributed to their economic success and to their continued dominance in the economic sphere. They are:

1. Commitment to work ethic;
2. Commitment to do their best in whatever they do. Give it 100%+ ;
3. Confidence that they can do anything as well as, if not better than, anyone else;
4. Competition is good and protection bad for society and individual.

These values are held to be essential to building a prosperous and caring society and a vast majority of people in these societies believe in and practise them in their daily lives. It is important to recognise that these are not religious values, although religion may have played a key role in the past in rationalising and promoting the work ethic and the commitment to do one's best to whatever one does etc., especially in Christian countries.

Work Ethic

What is work ethic? Can it be learned? Why is it so important in building a country? It can be defined in many ways but for our purpose we shall define it as " use of individual's time fully and productively in performance of activities which contribute to enrichment of human life". This includes enriching one's own life and it applies to time spent at work as well as at home. A person who believes in work ethic, when he is at work uses all his time productively to perform the assigned or contracted duties with conviction, and when at home uses the time to do useful things for himself and his family. Probably the best way most people can contribute to the betterment of human life would be by focusing on improving and enriching their own lives. Thus the first obligation is to apply work ethic to improve and enrich ones own family and its surroundings by using his/her time fully and productively at work and at home. When a vast majority in a society accepts this obligation and puts it into practice the society will automatically become enriched.

Work ethic is not necessarily an altruistic and religious concept although some religions tend to make it so. For example, some sects in Christianity believe that the only way one can serve God is through work. The only acceptable way to please God is by putting in a full day's work. Those who sit and while away precious time with idle chatter or sit and chant God's name all day while doing very little productive work invite the wrath of God. In other words the only way one can gain the acceptance of God is to work to improve oneself, or fellow human beings.

But most people in countries like the U.S.A, Japan, Germany etc. accept work ethic on its own merits. **If one does not use ones time to enrich human life what else is**

there to do? Nothing worthwhile! Any activity other than the one aimed at enriching human life would simply result in contributing to human misery. There is more misery, suffering, and unhappiness in those societies that do not believe in work ethic than in those which do. Human spirit is more liberating when one believes and practises work ethic than when one does not. The exhilarating feeling one gets when a person performs well at work or finishes a task such as painting a room, ploughing a field, cleaning a street, playing a game, helping a neighbour etc. is genuine and uplifting.

Work ethic combined with education and training would provide the members of a society with the tools necessary to pursue their work to the best of their abilities which, in turn, makes them highly productive. A productive society has a far better chance of achieving happiness and fulfilment than a non-productive or less productive one. It should be pointed out that education and training, without commitment to work ethic, is wasteful and dishonest. It is wasteful because the person has used up the resources of the society to acquire the education and training but is not prepared to contribute in return to the society. Dishonest because implicit in accepting the education and training is that the person would use it to better himself/herself or fellow human beings. This is a common problem in India. Many use their education and training to get a job but work as little as possible.

Until Japan's emergence as a super economic power, it looked as though the work ethic was found exclusively in only European races. It was tempting to conclude that it was unique to them and probably that it was a genetic trait. Japan has confounded these theories. It has proved that it is an acquired trait and not a genetic one. It can be learned by anyone if they are motivated to do so. For example, there are millions of Asian and African immigrants, many of them coming from societies which do not either believe in work ethic or are not consciously aware of it, living in Europe and North America. An overwhelming majority of them learn it in no time and become productive and happy citizens in their adopted countries. Particularly, immigrants from India do well in these countries. This is because they have the native intelligence and they readily understand the logic of work ethic and embrace it happily. No wonder many of them are very successful.

In India, a vast majority of Hindus do not believe in work ethic. Only the poor do, probably because without work they will be deprived of basic necessities such as food, shelter and clothing. It would seem then that it is a more or less grudging acceptance. But the real problem rests with the middle and rich classes of the society. The overwhelming majority of them see work, especially the physical work, as demeaning, undesirable, and something to avoid, if at all possible. They treat their jobs mainly as a source of income, power, and prestige. They work as little as possible both at their place of employment and at home and use any excuse to justify it. Very few believe in giving 100 per cent attention and energy to the job. Over the years Hindu society has come to believe that work is not something to enjoy but is something to put up with because one needs a source of income.

Work ethic is not just going to work place and returning home at appointed times. It is a positive attitude towards work both in and out of the work place. When at the work place one would ensure every minute is usefully spent. If on occasion when there is not enough work a person would help someone else who has more work than he can handle.

The time spent at the work place is time which, in fact, belongs to the employer. A person with the right attitude will make sure that the employer receives fully whatever he is entitled to without any reservation. This would be true even if the person is not very happy with the job for whatever reason. The person's attitude toward work does not change because he/she does not like the job or the employer. Belief in work ethic motivates a person to be fully productive at the work place no matter what the circumstances might be. Motivation is unconditional.

A similar attitude would persist at home, as well. For example, let us assume that a person does not have a job and is in search of one. More likely he would spend a lot more time at home than he would outside because, quite often, he would be waiting at home for responses from potential employers. A typical Hindu from a middle to rich classes of the society would not use that time at home doing something useful and meaningful for himself, or his family, or for his community. He usually whiles away the time with idle chatter accomplishing nothing rather than using it to build something useful or functional, such as improving the cleanliness or beauty of his surroundings or teaching his or neighbour's children some game and so on. There are always many worthwhile things one can do. But most Hindus would not bother because they either believe it is beneath them or it simply does not occur to them. A person who believes in work ethic behaves at home the same way he does at work place. He always finds something productive to do. Work ethic is a certain attitude towards life. A person who has it makes use of every moment of his/her life to do something worthwhile. It is compulsive attitude to use one's time productively.

In countries such as China, Korea, and Vietnam a vast majority of their population believes in and practises work ethic which is largely responsible for their rapid economic development. They have very little use for rhetoric.

Work is not part of the Hindu psyche, rhetoric is. Undoubtedly there is a small minority of Hindus who believe in and practise work ethic, but can the rest of them learn it and adopt it, as well ? As pointed out earlier, most, if not all, Hindus who migrate to Europe and North America readily embrace it. This proves that there should be no problem as far as learning is concerned. The real question then is whether the majority of Hindus in India would want to learn it? That largely depends on the intellectuals and opinion makers within the society. Some of them may argue that the concept is alien and not relevant to India. Others will likely invoke that worn out cliché that Hinduism survived 5000 years and there is no need for change now. But the majority of Hindus are sensible and given a proper explanation and understanding they would embrace it because it is logical and makes sense.

The importance of work ethic to economic development in India cannot be over emphasised. It impacts on the productivity of the nation and hence its competitiveness, which, in turn, determines the country's ability to eliminate poverty and improve standards of living of millions of its citizens.

Give it your best [100%+] to whatever you do

Sachin Tendulkar, Mohammad Azharuddin, Mahesh Bhupathi, and Leander Paes together would be better qualified to write this chapter. They would know from their own first hand experiences what it means to give 100%+. These men would not have been the great champions they are, if they do not give their respective sports 100%+ effort. If asked, they would tell us that improving ones performance is a never ending process and that when one is at the top there is no room for complacency for there is always someone around the corner getting ready to outdo him. These sports legends would also tell us that whatever else they may do they would try to do the same, that is, give it the best effort they possibly can. It becomes a habit with them. It would not be possible to turn it on when they play their game and turn it off the rest of the time. Giving 100%+ to everything they do would be part of their personality. They seek constant improvement and perfection in every thing they do, not just in their professional career.

The same principles apply in building a sound economy. Ability to compete both nationally and internationally is the key to success. The only thing that guarantees the success of an economy is the society that constantly seeks to improve its skills and in which people are disposed to giving their best performance [100%+ effort] to whatever they do. This is what helps the powerful economies of the world such as the U.S.A, Japan, and Germany keep abreast. Their societies are committed to giving their best to ensure that they stay ahead. It is hard to lose when a society is capable and determined to do the best it can in every thing it does.

If Hindus want India to develop a strong economy they need to cultivate the habit of giving their best to whatever they do, without reservation. We are not just talking about performance at place of employment, we are talking about anything and everything an individual does. It is a complete change of attitude. Whether one is playing a game, cleaning a street, gardening, dressing and making up, painting a house, helping a neighbour, keeping one's house and neighbourhood clean and beautiful, fighting a war, studying, rearing children, and so on, an individual makes it a habit of performing each task to the best of his/her ability. What does this mean and why should one do it?

Take for instance a person performing a task at a lower level than his skills and abilities allow him to; and let us assume this became a habit with him. He himself would be the first to know that he is performing below his potential and that he is under utilising his talents. It is difficult to imagine how a person can be proud of himself when he is deliberately under-performing. His self-dignity and self worth have to suffer; and eventually his sel-esteem and self-respect would be lost as well. When others around him find out what he is doing he will also lose their respect. Performing at 100% or better does not take extra time, but it does take extra care and concentration. The greater the concentration, the greater the quality of work. When a person produces quality work the feelings of accomplishment, satisfaction and pride that it generates are uplifting and gratifying. The person's self worth, self image, self-respect, and self-confidence are vastly enhanced. He would come to believe that given time and training he is capable of doing anything perfectly. What a difference it makes ? In the former situation he feels like a cheat and worthless and in the latter he feels like a winner who can take on the world!

When a person is giving his best to whatever he does, that means he is performing close to his limits. Doing this repeatedly he has the opportunity to push his limits farther every once in a while. When he does this more often he discovers that he can perform better than he thought he could. His confidence would justifiably sky rocket. Only when a person operates close to his limits, does he have the opportunity to push those limits farther and farther and thereby permanently enhance his performance. Thus the quality of work gets better and better all the time. It is an attitude that when one has it, is reflected in everything he does. The person exudes confidence that he can do anything and do it better. This attitude is prevalent in well developed societies such as the U.S.A, Germany, Japan, etc. Vast majority of their peoples give 100% or better to whatever they do and they enjoy doing it. This is perhaps a major reason why the economies of these countries produce, for the most part, the highest quality products in the world.

If India is ever to become a major economic power it has no choice but to try to build its economy based on quality. An essential prerequisite to produce quality products and services is a workforce which operates consistently to the best of their abilities giving 100%+ to whatever they do. Can India, especially Hindus develop such a motivated workforce?

There is nothing in Hindu culture today that advocates its followers to give their best in whatever they do. Many in the society are not even cognizant of this. The concept is completely new and alien to a vast majority of Hindus. Also some Hindu values work against the concept. More often than not Hindus value work based on power and prestige derived from it, they do not believe that all work is important, they consider mental work more important than physical work. Within the category of physical work the valuations are influenced by factors such as caste. Most Hindus do not appreciate that society is like an organism, everyone must work to keep it healthy and prosperous and that everybody's work is important in that respect. To appreciate this one needs to think of a city like Delhi functioning without garbage pick-up and sanitary workers for a couple of months. If some work is not considered important for reasons of caste, amount of salary, physical nature of the work etc. the persons who do the work will have very little motivation to give their best to their jobs. They would want to get by with as little effort as possible. No one can really blame them. Every human being wants his/ her work to be appreciated and considered important. The more they are appreciated the more they would be motivated to give it their best.

It should be pointed out that just because one wishes to give one's best to whatever one does, it does not mean one can automatically succeed in doing so. It is something that requires considerable training and practice in as many different situations and as often as possible. There is no substitute for practice and more practice. Thus it is a two-stage process. First, an individual needs to be convinced of the desirability of learning the habit of giving his best in everything he does. Second, there should be infrastructure facilities for him to learn and practise his skills.

The broad concept of work and its importance to mental and physical well-being are poorly understood and appreciated by Hindu society. Most fail to see the great spiritual uplift individuals receive in giving their best to every thing they do.

Confidence to do anything as well as, if not better, than anyone

Powerful economies can be built only when they are open to competition - domestic and foreign. When an economy is closed to competition there are not enough pressures to be efficient, low cost, and technologically innovative. Everyone except the owners and employees of the companies protected from competition suffer because of resulting inefficiencies and high prices. Particularly consumers suffer the most from the high prices, poor quality and service. This was clearly proven by communist economies prior to the collapse of the Soviet Union, and also by socialist economies such as India's prior to liberalisation. Competition is usually a good check on price growth. Many Indians have found that prices of TVs, cars, and various consumer goods have come down and quality and service have improved since liberalisation.

If a country wishes its economy to be one among the best, that is highly productive, low unit cost, and technologically up to date, the one and only way to achieve that is by opening the economy to full rigours of domestic as well as international competition. We do not want to turn this into a text book on economics, but wish to point out that an economy becomes stronger when it competes against the strong economies of the world. Right now, that is what South Korea, China and Taiwan are attempting to do. Germany, Japan, and the U.S economies are very strong because they compete vigorously in the international market. One of the reasons they do so successfully is that they not only have a well motivated work force, but more importantly they believe that they are the best in the world and are very confident that they can successfully compete against anyone else. Americans, Germans, Japanese exude confidence that they can do anything better than anyone. Whether or not they truly can is immaterial. What is important is that they believe they can. This gives them an enormous edge over others. Because of this confidence they constantly expose themselves to competition more than others which, in turn, helps them sharpen their skills and thus better able to compete and win. This cycle keeps on repeating. Psychologists tell us that a person has a better chance of succeeding if he believes he will than a person who does not.

If Hindus have any aspirations of turning India into an economic powerhouse, they have to show willingness, eagerness, and confidence to compete in both domestic and international markets. Ability to successfully compete does not come by merely wishing for it although it is a good first step. Skills, hard work, focus, and motivation to give 100%+ effort are essential ingredients for building confidence to successfully compete. Proper infrastructure facilities such as first class trade and vocational schools, polytechnics, and professional schools and colleges are necessary and critical for learning and sharpening skills. **Only the best preparation develops confidence and faith that that they can be as good as anyone**. It gradually strengthens as one learns to successfully compete step by step. This is a slow process but it can be done. Taiwan, South Korea and lately China have succeeded in building the confidence of their citizens that they can successfully compete in international markets. This, they are doing by providing first class training to their workers and forcing their economies to compete globally.

There is no other way to develop the confidence of an individual that he can do anything as well as anyone can except through competition. One can successfully compete only by undergoing first class training and preparation. A society that does not strive to give its citizens the best training, as good as can be found anywhere in the world, does not have a hope that it can compete successfully against the best.

Many of the Hindu elite love to believe that India is as capable as any in the world and that their country should be treated as an emerging economic power on equal footing with China. No doubt this is a logical aspiration. But China deliberately and convincingly engages itself in competition with the West and Japan in all fields [i.e. economics, trade, politics, sports, culture etc.] which gives it a greater chance of becoming at least equal to them, if not better than them. India, on the other hand, behaves like it is not sure of itself and is afraid to come out of its shell. It puts one foot out the door, takes a look around for a while and then pulls back into the shell. Ability to compete with the best does not come easy. It is hard work and it is for ever more demanding. To want to compete must become a well-ingrained habit, otherwise it is not enjoyable. One cannot approach it on an on and off basis. That is a sure way to destroy self-confidence and lose out in the long run.

If Hindus really want to transform themselves and their country to become internationally competitive, they will have to develop and build an appropriate infrastructure to impart first class training to their citizens in various skills and also help inculcate competitive values and spirit in every aspect of life. Only then they will develop confidence to believe that they can compete with the best in the world. There is no substitute for preparation and training.

Competition is Good and Protection Bad

Citizens of the most economically developed societies believe that competition is vital to the economy in order to keep it healthy and dynamic. It motivates businesses to be efficient and forces them to do research and development in order to discover and perfect new technologies which will improve their operations and products, and to design new products so that they can successfully compete. Competition forces a company to become as, if not more, efficient as its competitors in all aspects of its operations including marketing, sales, finance, manufacturing, distribution, product development and so on. The sole purpose of efficiency is to reduce unit costs and improve service which in turn result in lower prices and better service to customers. When prices are lowered more people can afford to buy the product creating more demand for it which in turn creates more jobs. This is the reason economists say that competition maximizes demand, output, and employment. Conversely, lesser the competition fewer the jobs.

There is no better way to alleviate poverty and improve standard of living of a society than by maximizing employment opportunities for the masses which can be done only by opening up the economy for more competition. For example the U.S. economy is the most competitive economy in the world and hence it has one of the lowest unemployment rates among the developed societies. Since the United Kingdom moved away from its socialist policies and opened up its economy to more competition, the employment opportunities in that country have dramatically improved in recent years. Many Europeans are going there to find jobs.

The same principles apply with respect to global economy The more competition the more employment growth among the world economies. The East and South East Asian countries expanded employment opportunities for their citizens by opening up their economies for competition and also by successfully competing in the global markets which in turn helped to dramatically reduce poverty in these countries.

Similar experiences can be found in India; for example, take the automobile industry which has become highly competitive since the liberalisation of the economy. Car prices have dropped allowing more people the affordability to buy cars creating a growing demand for the product and, hence, output and employment have been expanding as well.

Another advantage of competition is that people become more disciplined and develop a winning attitude because it forces employees to be on their toes and to perform as best as they possibly can on their jobs, otherwise their employer may not overcome the rigours of competition in which case everyone will lose his or her job. The society becomes more efficiency oriented in all aspects of life thus contributing to greater productivity. Earlier it was mentioned that competition forces businesses to develop new technologies to retain their competitive edge. When this becomes widespread in the economy, the nation will develop skills and dexterity to use the technology to solve other problems in the society as well.

Why then the Indian government and politicians are slow, if not reluctant, to fully open up the economy and promote intense competition? The reasons are several fold. Some companies oppose it because they are afraid that competition will put pressure on their profitable businesses. Others oppose because they are afraid that competition will only make it worse for their current unprofitable businesses and so on. The point to remember is that no company will welcome more competition unless it is well managed by world standards. There may be some short term pain for employees of those companies which cannot compete and therefore fail, but in the long run new and efficient companies will rise from the ashes of failed ones and create more jobs. It is in the best interest of the society that inefficient companies do fail.

Some politicians oppose competition out of sheer ignorance. Many Indian politicians do not know or understand the basic principles of economics due to lack of exposure and very little experience in governance. But they are afraid to admit that they do not know and learn. Instead they make irresponsible remarks which cause fear in the minds of innocent citizens; and also they promote ideas and policies that would ruin the country. Take for example George Fernandes of the Samata Party; he has been getting carried away with his dislike and disapproval of allowing multinational corporations to operate in the consumer product markets in India. His perennial favourite targets are Coca Cola and Pepsi Cola, along with some others. Let us analyse this.

Indian businessmen developed a good soft drink industry in India. But per capita consumption of soft drinks in the country is far behind compared to many developing countries. That would imply that either the existing Indian companies are not growing fast enough to satisfy the demand, or that the prices are high and many people cannot afford to buy them at all or as frequently as they would like. This means prices need to come down so that more consumers can afford to buy the product which would happen only when there is more competition in the industry. Someone might say the price of Coca Cola and Pepsi Cola are usually higher than the local brands and therefore their presence will not contribute to increase in demand. On the contrary it would, because when some consumers switch to foreign brands, for whatever reason, the demand for local brands suffers forcing local companies to drop their prices in order to maintain their volume of business. Thus some of the people who could not afford to buy at all or as frequently before can do so now. Thus when there is more competition, more people will be able to buy the product and more jobs are created in the industry.

Some would argue that these multinational companies like Coca Cola simply buy out local companies and contribute very little to the development of economy. Again this is a wrong conclusion. A local businessman who sold his business to them can now use the proceeds from that sale to start up another business in the same or other industry and thus create more jobs. Total investment in the economy would therefore increase and that in turn would expand the number of jobs in the economy. In addition, multinational corporations bring with them better technology and management, forcing competitors to learn and adopt the same thereby making the entire industry more efficient.

Another common slogan is that India needs foreign companies to invest in manufacturing computer chips, not potato chips. This again is a misconception. Does India produce enough potato chips today so that anyone can purchase them in quantities he or she likes? The answer is no; there are so many poor people who would like to buy but cannot afford to. Any objective minded Indian will agree that there is not a single product produced in the economy enough to satisfy the needs of all Indians in quantities they would like to enjoy at prices they can afford. Therefore what India needs in the foreseeable future is investment with no bounds which would create more and more jobs. It is cruel and unfair to the poor and the unemployed to discourage investment whatever the excuse might be. Poor need jobs desperately. Private investment flows freely and in huge quantities into open and fully competitive markets. India can never afford to borrow capital in the amounts required to invest in its economy in order to create millions of jobs required. If it is really serious about eliminating poverty within a reasonable period of time, say 20 years, it simply cannot do it without huge quantities of private and foreign investment.

The belief, in developed societies, that competition is good, is based on experience not just theories. They realise that the standard of living enjoyed by all in their societies is mostly attributable to their competitive economies. They know that protecting their economies from domestic and/or foreign competition would only make them inefficient resulting in high prices and reduced employment.

Some people advocate having a fully competitive domestic economy but they want to protect it from foreign competition. If every country follows this practice the export opportunities will dry up for everyone which would result in shrinking economies worldwide. If a country unfairly restricts imports then other countries will retaliate in kind which would only make things worse. But an economy becomes much more efficient when it is exposed to global competition resulting in lower prices and more investment than would otherwise be the case. Protection may help a particular company, but it hurts the economy and the poor because it results in higher prices and reduced investment and fewer employment opportunities.

The values discussed in this section are crucial to developing economic and competitive attitudes in people for building a strong economy capable of competing globally. Once a society acquires these attitudes it is hard to lose no matter what challenges it may be faced with. Economies built with armies of unskilled and semi-skilled workers without the society changing its fundamental values related to work would be like building a house without a foundation. Some of the Arab countries are attempting to do this. These societies will have trouble to cope once the oil based wealth is depleted. On the other hand, Germany which was reduced to rubble during the second world war was able to build one of the most powerful economies in the world out of that rubble in less than 20 years. How did this happen? Germans have had the fundamental values and skills needed to build a strong economy which no one could take away from them. This is a clear testament to the power of values.

Chapter 4

Social Values

Social values determine the interactions among members of a society and their orientation and motivation to non-religious aspects of life. There is obviously some overlap between social and religious values, but that is not of critical importance for our purpose. Usually cultural and religious evolution, historical experiences of the society, and geography have significant bearing on the evolution of these values. These social values, in conjunction with religious values largely determine the character of individuals in a society. Their influence is inescapable unless one is determined to deny them.

Certain social values are common to all developed societies. They give stimulus to their development and would be applicable to any society aspiring for the same. These values are basic and have very little religious connotation. One can find that these values are being adopted by the fast developing societies of East and South east Asian countries, as well. These are:

1. Commitment to economic and social development.
2. Attention to detail and observation before generalising, philosophising, and judging.

3. Strengthening of individual.
4. Respect for fellow human beings. Recognise some good in every human being.
5. Dignity of work.
6. Commitment to cleanliness.
7. Orientation for accomplishment.

Each one of these values has a bearing on how a society develops and matures into a progressive one.

Commitment to Economic and Social Development

As obvious as this is, a society has to have a strong commitment to economic and social development for it to be able to achieve it. In developed societies such as the USA, Canada, and the UK the commitment is almost like a religion. They believe that it is the natural right of individuals to seek to better themselves in every aspect of life, especially economic and social aspects. They adopt and adjust to whatever may be necessary to accomplish this. Most of their values are shaped to motivate themselves to improve their lot in life. These societies unify and work to achieve basic economic goals of providing a job for everyone that needs one so that his family can have the basic necessities of life which would enable them to live with dignity and security. They are highly motivated to develop strong economies which can provide jobs and a high standard of living.

Developed societies are also committed to social justice for all their citizens which they believe would be easier to achieve if everyone who needs a job can find one. They focus first on building a strong economy which can provide jobs and resources to solve many social problems because they recognise that it is very difficult to achieve social justice in a society where most people do not have jobs.

Developing countries such as China, South Korea, Singapore, Taiwan, and so on have adopted a similar commitment to economic and social development. Their citizens adopt necessary values and contribute in whatever way they can to help speed up economic development so that they can all have jobs and better standard of living.

Due to the considerable illiteracy in the Hindu society, many of its citizens do not realise that they have the right to seek a better life, and that their society is capable of providing jobs and a better standard of living for everyone, if it were to adopt appropriate development values and a commitment to doing whatever is necessary to build a strong economy. As a result of this ignorance, there is no overwhelming demand and commitment among all citizens for economic and social development. Also, the Hindu religion has never encouraged its followers to aggressively work to liberate themselves from poverty. On the contrary it has always rationalised acceptance of poverty. Thus illiteracy and religion together have been holding back many Hindus from aggressively demanding their fundamental right to jobs and a better standard of living. Many of them do not realise that social justice usually follows when the economic justice of providing a job to whoever needs one is realised.

Politicians will focus on building a rapidly growing economy only when they sense a vast majority of the population is committed to it and demands it.

Attention to Detail

One of the trademarks of Hindus is that they are quick to judge, generalise, and philosophise before a clear understanding of issues. Most Hindus make liberal use of adjectives such as good, bad, beautiful, ugly, smart, stupid, rich, poor, etc. They are quick to use these adjectives and show very little desire for probing, questioning, and describing. Most of them have trouble describing things clearly and in detail as they do not spend time and effort to observe and collect all details pertaining to an incident, phenomenon, person, or thing. For example, many of them will have trouble to describe a tree in front of their home in more than three or four sentences. If one were to ask to write an essay describing it in no less than two pages, very few would be able to do it. But they can tell you in one second whether they like the tree or not and whether it is a good or bad tree.

I recall watching an interview once on a Canadian TV programme. A very well known Indian movie actress was being interviewed and the interviewer asked her what she thought of another famous Indian actor. She answered "he is good, very good" shaking her head left to right several times. But she did not or could not point out what makes him good. She was unable to point out one single characteristic about him that she thought was good. This is very typical of a vast majority of Hindus. For example, they have trouble explaining why they vote for a certain candidate in elections. Indian journalists interviewing politicians and other popular figures is another example. The questions and answers lack specificity and pertinent details required for better understanding, thorough evaluation, valid conclusion, and to form an informed opinion. Why is this so important in nation building? Some would argue that this is simply knit-picking and has no relevance to great issues of nation building whatsoever.

What makes a society great is its people; not the government, not the politicians, not the physical resources. The strength of its people depends not only on their physical well-being but also on their ability to gather and process information. This attribute is the only basis for proper understanding of issues and informed decisions both at individual and society level. A correctly informed citizen is an invaluable asset for nation building.

In countries such as the U.S.A, the U.K, Germany, and Canada, it is the average citizen that makes the achievements of these countries possible, not the elite. Individual citizens are well informed, and hence well motivated to take active part in building their societies. Ordinary citizens play a vital and dominant role in all aspects of life. Whether it is in sports, commerce, politics, science, health, social issues, religion, or education, individual initiatives play a leading role in understanding issues clearly, the forming of opinions, and eventually forcing their governments to develop and implement policies consistent with public opinion. What are the unique characteristics of these people that makes this possible? A vast majority of people in these societies pay attention to detail and collect as much detailed information as possible before they judge, generalise and conclude. Going back to the example discussed earlier, most of these people have the ability to describe a tree in front of their house in two pages or better because they observe everything, paying attention to minute details and asking themselves why something is the way it is. When one listens to people in these societies it is immediately striking of how detail minded they really are, how well they pay attention to detail and how reluctant they are to generalise, philosophise, and judge. Quite often they describe but refrain from concluding for as long as they can. In answer to a question some people describe all relevant factors in detail but let the questioner conclude. As a result they have a better chance of identifying as many facts as possible before drawing firm conclusions.

A society or an individual who does not have the ability or does not bother to seek out all the relevant facts is not in a position to draw correct conclusions, to arrive at a correct judgment on issues and hence is likely to fail in understanding and resolving issues as best as they can be. Most irrational fears and prejudices are attributable to lack of correct understanding of issues which in turn relates back to lack of attention to detail. Hindus fear of multinational corporations, prejudices pertaining to justification of caste, and childhood marriages are some examples of this.

More often than not conclusions based on vague generalities do not withstand the test of detailed analysis. Most business people and research professionals can attest to this. This is the reason for the saying in the Western world "generalities are great, but the devil is in the detail". Take for example, following the nuclear tests by India and Pakistan in May 1998 the Prime Minister Mr. Vajpayee offered Pakistan to sign a "no-first use" agreement - meaning neither country would use nuclear weapons first on the other in any war between the two countries. Presumably, if one uses them first then the other has the right to retaliate in kind. Let us analyse this. Nuclear weapons can cause massive destruction and usually couple of medium sized bombs would be enough to bring any country to its knees, and after that the country may not be in a position to retaliate in kind at all. Pakistanis and Indians do not trust each other,. whatsoever. Pakistani military establishment still has control over the politics and politicians in that country, and it can easily override the politicians and explode half a dozen nuclear weapons, all at once, on India in any future conflict between the two countries. Does Mr. Vajpayee really believe India can retaliate following such a devastation? What good that will do? Mr. Vajpayee's reckless proposal to sign "no-first use" agreement can only be attributed to his lack of attention to detail and detailed analysis.

If Hindus want to succeed in building a progressive society based on strong individuals, they must learn to observe and to pay more attention to detail in every aspect of life. Detailed information strengthens individual. To begin with they must learn to describe everything in great detail and resist the temptation to generalise, philosophise, and judge prematurely. In addition they should cultivate the habit of answering questions with lot of details and learn to be more precise and descriptive of everything. For example, try to refrain from saying that so and so is a good person. Instead say, he helps neighbours [if that is true] or he never steals, he contributes to charities, whatever may be relevant. Also when a person is speaking in generalities, it is a good idea for the listener to ask for specifics. When a person says so and so is a bad person ask him politely to explain why he believes and lead him on to be more specific and descriptive.

It is not difficult to learn to pay attention to detail and to be descriptive. One has to consciously work at it everyday all day for a couple of months until it becomes a habit. One should try to describe every thing in as much detail as possible i.e. people, things, and situations. Within a few days the person can notice the difference. It becomes a habit within a short period of time to observe minute details and ask detailed questions about everything. It is easier to teach children than adults because they have more curiosity, ask more questions and are genuinely interested in learning. Most adult habits are well-ingrained and take a little more time and effort to change.

Attention to detail means asking a lot of questions pertaining to the subject matter, never stopping until completely satisfied with the amount and accuracy of detail, never concluding or generalising unless it is absolutely required. The benefits of this to individual and society cannot be over-emphasised. Progress and motivation for change stem from questioning everything around us. One can show direct correlation between this and the level of development of a society. The more citizens are detail minded, the more progressive the society would become. Decisions will be made based on detailed understanding of facts instead of slogans and prejudices.

Strengthening of Individual

In developed societies such as the USA, the UK, and Canada the individual is treated as autonomous and his rights are carefully balanced against those of society and government. Every citizen is made to feel that his needs and aspirations are as important as those of the society and there are limits beyond which society and government cannot encroach on his rights and freedoms. These societies genuinely believe that strengthening of individual leads to strengthening of society. They also recognise that strong societies are built with strong individuals and a society cannot become strong by weakening the individual however hard it may try. To illustrate this point let us take the example of former communist countries. In those societies, the governments kept all rights and individuals were granted only a few, and even those could be taken away at the discretion of the governments. Therefore the societies consisted of individuals with very few rights. Unless one believes government and society are the same, those societies were as weak as individuals in it. Where does the strength of the society stem from? It is important to recognise that government is not society but only purports to act on its behalf. Strong government does not mean strong society; it usually means weak society consisting of weak individuals. Only when an individual has strong rights does the society have the same. When a society works to strengthen the individual it is in effect strengthening itself.

Developed societies strengthen their citizens in other ways besides ensuring that they have strong individual rights. They build proper infrastructure facilities such as well-equipped schools and sports facilities to enable their citizens to learn skills to prepare them for jobs and/or develop their talents in sports etc. Night schools are operated for their convenience offering varieties of programmes to learn new skills or to update old skills. No efforts are spared to help those citizens who want to better themselves.

When there is a high degree of focus on strengthening the individual, he develops enormous self-confidence which encourages him to work to reach his full potential. Since he sees the society is working to strengthen him, in turn, he will be motivated to work to strengthen the society by participating in activities such as community caring and development programmes. This is clearly evident in developed societies.

Hindu culture has not focused much on the development of individuals, at least not over the past one thousand years. The individual's interests have always been readily subordinated to those of society and government without much care and discussion, and also there have never been concerted efforts to build adequate infrastructure facilities to enable all citizens to develop their abilities and talents.

Since independence the Central Government has focused more on strengthening the power of bureaucrats than the rights of its citizens. Many politicians mistakenly believe that strengthening of government is tantamount to strengthening of society. They are against transferring power from the Central Government to citizens because they are afraid that it will weaken the society, and also they do not have confidence that citizens are capable of making correct decisions. This is also a major reason why politicians do not want to decentralise power of the Central Government to the provinces and local communities. They do not understand that society cannot become strong when citizens are kept weak. As a result an average citizen lacks self-confidence and is uncertain of his role in the development of his community and of his country. Also there is not enough focus on building proper infrastructure facilities to develop the talents of all citizens. Countries like China have been doing a much better job in this respect than India.

The most obvious consequence of keeping citizens and society weak is that the responsibility for economic development of the country primarily rests in the hands of bureaucrats, who would steer the economy in the direction which would only strengthen their power not weaken it. This can be clearly seen in the bureaucrats attempts to frustrate tatas from getting into Airline industry and building airports.

Hindus should recognise that it is not possible to speed up the economic development or to develop India into an international power by keeping their citizens and society weak. Only a strong society based on strong individuals makes it possible.

Respect for Fellow Human Beings and Their Rights

In developed societies it is clearly noticeable that people respect and appreciate each other's abilities and their contributions to improve themselves and the society. People, for the most part concentrate on the positive side of fellow human beings and shy away from judging another person's faults and/or weaknesses unless they hurt others. Sensitivity and respect for the rights of fellow human beings is common and is expected from one another it is also a legal requirement. What this does is to not only ensure social peace and security, but also enhances civility and motivation of individuals to better themselves and the society. It enhances co-operative spirit of citizens which in turn enables the society to set for itself demanding goals and to successfully achieve them.

In Hindu society, respect for authority and the rich is prevalent as is the case in many societies. But what differentiates them is that they have very little regard or respect for those who lack power and/or wealth. This is in direct conflict with Hindus' professed claim that they are a non-materialistic people. Also it is very well known that Hindus judge people by their caste. A person's caste has a significant bearing on his/her standing within the society. But power and wealth override caste more often than not. If a low caste person has power and/or wealth he or she is readily accorded social acceptance.

Hindus lack respect and sensitivity for the rights of fellow citizens. Perhaps this was due to a long period of subjugation under Mogul and British rule, a caste based social structure, and an average Hindu's lack of desire or ability to observe, question, change, and progress. The subjugation contributed to loss of self-respect among Hindus because the masters despised everything about them. It is impossible to respect another human being when one is devoid of self-respect. This was one of the greatest tragedies of foreign rule. It not only destroyed self-respect of Hindus but it also accentuated the worst aspects of the caste system. Loss of self-respect on the part of upper castes intensified their disrespect for lower castes and insensitivity to their rights. Over time this has become deeply ingrained into their way of life. Even today in modern India, lower caste citizens and untouchables are maimed and murdered in provinces such as Bihar, Madhya Pradesh and Utter Pradesh. Hindu society as a whole never feels indignant enough to send troops to capture and punish those who commit such crimes. These atrocities do not seem to offend the heart and soul of the Hindu establishment.

Why is it so important to respect and be sensitive to the rights of fellow human beings? What has this to do with developing and securing India? It is a monumental and complex task, to say the least, to build and secure a country like India. It depends on the motivation and will of all its people to make the necessary adjustments and sacrifices. Social justice and peace are an important prerequisite to a rapid and lasting economic growth. Why would lower castes and untouchables who from the time of birth are treated as inferior want to contribute to building a society that would perpetuate and reinforce their unjust, unappreciative, and degrading position in the society? If large segments of the population are indifferent or opposed to the social system because of social injustices perpetuated on them, or the fruits of development are not shared in a just manner, the country's efforts to develop will be derailed or considerably slowed. It is therefore in the larger interest of the society to treat all its citizens as equal. A society operates at its best and is capable of achieving its maximum potential when all its citizens and their contributions are appreciated and treated as equal.

Given training and opportunity every human being is capable of achievement and contribution. Higher caste Hindus who currently enjoy privileged positions were simply fortunate enough to get their training; their caste has very little to do with their ability. The caste may have given them undue advantage of access to training. An individual without training from an upper caste cannot be any better than an individual without training from a lower caste. Both would be equally ignorant.

There is nothing more inhuman and outrageous than telling a fellow human being that he or she is inferior because of his or her caste, race, or religion. It far exceeds any cruelty one can imagine. The incalculable damage that it would do to the self-respect and self-esteem and therefore to the self-confidence of the individual, has never been understood by the upper caste Hindus. Many of them don't even care. In such circumstances there is no way a person from lower caste would grow up respecting the world around him/her. He or she would not be able to see any point in respecting others and their rights when their own rights are violated. One cannot find fault with that person. Most people in this predicament would want to lash out at the society at every opportunity. They would be least motivated to bettering a society which in turn tells them that they are inferior. Why should they bother? A majority of Hindus are from a lower caste which means that the priority of this majority is not economic development but social development and acceptance. Therefore, unless there is a vast improvement in social matters the country will have difficulty in achieving a higher rate of economic growth. Recent United Nations studies have shown that India is one among the lowest ranking countries in human development and ranks much lower than Southeast and East Asian countries. This cannot be surprising to Hindus. The upper caste Hindus who control the power in India simply do not place the necessary priorities and focus in removing the social barriers facing the lower caste and providing them with the necessary training programmes to teach them skills on a massive scale. They seem to give higher priority in having government continue investing scarce resources in companies such as Maruti Udyog and other PSUs even after the economy is liberalised.

The caste system has been perpetuated for thousands of years because of lack of desire and commitment to self-evaluation and improvement on the part of Hindu society. The Hindu establishment was unable or unwilling to take note of the psychological damage and suffering that the caste system was inflicting on the lower caste citizens. It is still the same today. No one in the establishment cares enough to systematically analyse the problem using modern tools to educate the public on the effects of the caste system on human development. There has been no massive effort to reverse the psychological damage that the caste system causes. And nothing is in the works, either. When a society allows suppression of rights of a segment of its citizens it risks losing everyone's rights.

Consistent rapid economic development is possible when there is sensitivity and respect for human rights of everyone in the society. It promotes harmony and co-operation among citizens which makes it easy for the country to achieve its fundamental and challenging goals of economic development and national security.

Dignity of Work

Earlier we have alluded to the fact that most Hindus lack dignity of work. This is mainly attributable to their caste system which in the past assigned certain work to certain castes. The name lower caste is derived from the fact that they are assigned low end jobs such as street cleaning, domestic work, barbering etc. which are considered undesirable and therefore upper castes attach a stigma to these jobs. It is almost correct to say that the hatred and disrespect of upper castes for the lower castes is based on the fact that the latter perform the jobs considered by upper castes to be filthy and undesirable. For them, lower caste is synonymous with dirty and undesirable work. Over the centuries upper castes have successfully avoided doing the work of lower castes because they consider it insulting to their own caste. The Hindus have always graded the respectability of work based on these biases. They never believed in dignity of work because they could not bring themselves to accept that the work performed by the lower castes was dignified. This gradually spread to dislike of almost all physical work regardless of whether it was originally assigned to the lower caste or not. For example, this is one of the reasons most Hindus shun even occupations such as nursing. There is now some relaxation of some of these beliefs, but not much has changed.

What is dignity of work? Why is it so important to building a nation ? A society that believes in dignity of work, respects and values the contribution of every citizen for the betterment of the society. A citizen contributes to society primarily by looking after himself and his family, by holding a job or running a business, or by doing something useful for the society. There are almost an unlimited number of tasks required to be done everyday for society to run smoothly and prosper. These range from cleaning the streets, growing food, manufacturing clothes, flying airplanes, fighting a war, cleaning clothes, cooking food, rearing children etc. From the society point of view everyone of these jobs needs to be done, otherwise somebody or other will suffer or be inconvenienced. It would be impossible to rank all these jobs as to their importance. Only when everyone does their job does the society run smoothly. In that respect all jobs are important. A janitor's work is as important to the society as anybody else's. Just because it is a low paying job, does not mean it is unimportant. A person's income has very little to do with the importance of his/her contribution to the society. Dr. Einstein made very little money compared to a medical doctor, a business executive, or even a good plumber but his contributions were more far reaching than those of any human being ever born on this earth. Generally, people who pursue solely money will make more money than others. e.g. business people. That does not follow that their contribution to the society is better than others. From the society's point of view all these jobs need to be accomplished and they are therefore equally important. How can a society be happy and healthy when the streets are not cleaned, garbage is not picked up etc. Can a society survive without farmers doing their work? And so on. Everybody's work is important and that is why everyone deserves to be treated with dignity and respect. Hence the dignity of work.

Dignity of work leads to dignity of human beings and vice versa. It empowers the society to accomplish its goals and objectives and reach its potential when all its citizens feel that their contributions are recognised and valued. A society cannot tell one citizen that his work is less valuable than another and still hope to accomplish its objectives and prosper. It would be suicidal for it to engage in that kind of behaviour.

In developed societies such as the U.S.A everyone in the society takes pride in their work and also respect the work of others no matter what it is. People who are lazy and do not care to work are the ones who receive very little or no respect. Garbage collectors, janitors, and household workers etc. are treated with the same dignity and courtesy as any other worker. In doing their job well everyone feels that they are doing their part for the society for it to function smoothly. This devotion to dignity of work and dignity of individual in the United States society empowers it to set for itself the most difficult and challenging goals knowing that its citizens will do their part to help it to achieve them.

If India is to develop into a strong economic power, then Hindus must change their ways and accept dignity of work. It is also the most human thing to do. No human being has the right to strip another person's dignity no matter what the pretext may be. A caring society believes in restoring it.

Cleanliness

India may well be the filthiest and dirtiest of any civilised country in the world. Its slums and unattended open sewers all across the country with only a few exceptions defy logic, understanding, and more importantly human dignity. One cannot put the blame for this solely on poverty. Many poor countries such as China, Vietnam, Indonesia, Thailand, even prior to the last fifteen years of their economic growth were much cleaner than India is today. Only the poorest of the poor African countries are filthier. What is even more amazing is that the Hindu establishment is not offended by it, and therefore they are not motivated enough to act! Why is this so? The colonial past has something to do with it. Colonial masters [both Moguls and British] confiscated properties owned by Hindus under one pretext or another and forced them to live in poverty, filth and squalor. Public health issues were not attended to in areas where Hindus resided. But even that does not fully explain it. Keeping one's surroundings clean is not always expensive or the responsibility of government alone. If Hindus had the desire and the will to keep their surroundings clean there was nothing preventing them from doing so. No doubt, their rulers had no desire to spend money for the up keep of Hindu areas, but they would not have made those areas purposefully filthy if Hindus had tried to keep them clean on their own. Therefore, Hindu culture and attitude had a great deal to do with it as well.

It has been noted earlier that Hindu culture has never promoted community values and spirit and therefore Hindus never acquired them in any significant way. It is more or less the same today. Community problems such as public health, hygiene, street maintenance, sanitation and sewers, community safety and security etc. require local initiatives and involvement. Even under the best of circumstances central and provincial governments can only do so much for a local community without active involvement by the community itself. As a result, community needs get little attention unless there is strong local initiative. When government is colonial and repressive, community matters will not receive any sympathetic hearing whatsoever. This was what happened under Mogul and British rule. Community issues were ignored by governments. And the local communities did not try to do their part either. The poverty conditions imposed on Hindus by the Moguls contributed to further deterioration of their areas and attracted filth and squalor. Hindus did little to prevent it.

Conditions today have not improved much, either. Hindus still lack strong community values and spirit. The governments are inefficient and corrupt. Community development hardly receives the commitment, focus, resources, and attention required from either the locals or from governments to sufficiently make a dent on local issues such as sanitation, sewers, street maintenance, etc. Therefore filth and squalor continue to flourish.

Since there are no social or religious organisations which can bring a local community together on a regular basis it would be difficult to inculcate the necessary community values among the population. There is no doubt most Hindus keep their houses very clean. But they display little interest or desire to work to keep their streets or the villages clean and beautiful. Filth and squalor on the streets rarely moves them to action. Their imagination does not extend beyond the perimeter of their own homes. They rarely think, for example, that they would like to see their village to be the cleanest and the most beautiful in their district or that they would like to make their street the cleanest and the prettiest in the village. For that matter you don't hear anyone expressing a desire to make India one of the cleanest and the most beautiful countries in the world. When there is no expressed desire for change, it rarely happens.

No doubt, there are village and town councils in communities across India, but ordinary citizens rarely look upon them as effective instruments of change. There is very little participation by them in the operation of these councils, and in most cases they also lack resources and good leadership. Creating a beautiful and clean village or town is a community affair. When there is no community spirit these things just do not happen. This lack of community spirit among Hindus, combined with their insensitivity to filth and squalor, has resulted in a country which has been and still is the filthiest and the dirtiest in the civilised world.

One may ask why is this so important? Why can't India be dirty and filthy and still become economically strong and aspire to become a world power? A human being is in harmony with nature when he/she lives in clean and beautiful surroundings. Self-worth and self-dignity are enhanced, the human spirit is uplifted, which in turn significantly improves the productivity of the individual. Filthy surroundings depress the human spirit, signify the defeat of the spirit and the acceptance of it. A society that accepts defeat in an important matter such as public health will find it easy to do the same in other important matters as well.

Also, the purpose of economic development is to improve the material well-being of citizens of a country including public health and the environment. If Hindus do not include the elimination of filth and squalor among them as a part of their economic development, then they are, in effect, saying to the world that for them economic development means only the production of cars, TVs, refrigerators, fancy clothes etc. and does not include improving the environment around them. I am sure most of them do not mean it.

Many Hindus aspire for India to become a major economic and political power to reckon with in the not too distant future. Can this happen? Most peoples of the world automatically believe that clean and beautiful countries are superior to those that are not, in their outlook and ability to change the environment to enrich human life. Also, the civility and maturity of a society is reflected in the cleanliness and beauty of its surroundings. A society that aspires to becoming either a regional power or one of the world powers must show that it has the ability and stamina to take control of its problems and solve them. If India is not offended and revolted by the filth and squalor that predominates its landscape like cancer, and is unable to take control of the problem and solve it then one can say that the society is not only dehumanised but it is also unfit for leadership of any kind on the world scene.

All developed countries without exception put enormous emphasis on keeping their countries clean and beautiful. Mostly local communities take responsibility for this. Even fast developing countries such as China, Malaysia, and Thailand devote considerable effort and resources in ensuring their countries are clean and beautiful, consistent with their growing affluence.

If Hindus want to see India join the ranks of civilised countries and become a major world power they need to prove to themselves, and the world, that they have the capacity to transform their country into a clean and beautiful place. But it cannot be done by the Central Government alone. The society needs to develop first community spirit and pride. Then resources should be made available to local communities and local governments so that they can take control of the problem and solve it for themselves. Also, many countries organise national campaigns to clean up their cities and villages, and keep them clean. Why can't India do something similar?

Orientation for Tangible Accomplishment

In economically advanced countries most people orient their lives around activities that, when successfully completed, give them a sense of accomplishment and satisfaction. These activities are in addition to their regular jobs. They could cover such things as raising funds for worthy causes, volunteering time to help community service organisations, playing favourite sports and games, fixing and improving their homes e.g. painting the house, and so on. Many of these activities not only contribute to improving the quality of life for themselves and their community but they also help in sharpening their skills and abilities in organising and doing certain tasks which they would otherwise not have. Thus the people are constantly engaged in activities which give them a sense of accomplishment and in turn improves their self-worth, productivity, and their competitive ability.

Hindus are more rhetoric than accomplishment oriented. Their tendency is to talk themselves out of action whenever they possibly can. Sometimes they even confuse rhetoric as action. Religion probably has a lot to do with it. It is more inward looking and emphasises more on renouncing worldly duties than doing one's best to build himself/herself an enjoyable and happy life. The focus is on performing more non-material activities such as prayers which, it is hoped, will please God more than by doing things which would make life better here on earth. Treating oneself as nothing before God is encouraged and justified. Believing that God considers the life of every human being as important and valuable is shunned and thus interpreted as arrogance. Over the centuries this has led to emphasising intellectual pursuits, not directly related to improving material life, such as mathematics, philosophy etc. It is not surprising that Hindus tend to be better in these types of pursuits. But basically the above beliefs did very little to boost self-esteem, self-worth, and the competitive spirit of individuals. It denied motivation for individuals to orient themselves for accomplishing material things which make life enjoyable.

As well, these beliefs have held Hindus back from celebrating and glorifying human life and spirit, and their potential to unlock the secrets of the universe for the betterment of the human race. They could never bring themselves to build such monuments as the Taj Mahal to celebrate one human being's love for another because that would have been considered a vulgar display of human emotions and spirit.

Hindus have never valued individualism and many still don't. Their values do not encourage individuals to believe that they can make a difference. They fail to recognise that when an individual is strong the society becomes strong as well. One cannot build a strong wall with weak bricks and the same applies in society's case. Even today the political and social system is not geared to strengthening the individual and orienting him/her for greater accomplishment and achievement. It treats individual citizens as if they don't matter, and is always ready to sacrifice their interests to those of society without giving proper consideration to careful balance. This is certainly not the way to build and enhance the self-esteem and confidence of an individual and orient him for accomplishment and success.

In advanced countries the political, legal, and social systems work to remove obstacles in the way of an individual and facilitate the full liberation and blossoming of human spirit. Individuals in these societies believe that they can, and do, make a difference and have full confidence in their abilities to do so. They are encouraged to develop self-respect, dignity, esteem, and confidence and to reinforce these they are provided with facilities and opportunities to compete and sharpen their abilities and skills.

If India wishes to develop into a significant economic and political force in the international arena, it must free the individual and encourage him/her to believe that he/she can make a difference, by removing all impediments in his or her way. The society should learn to celebrate human achievements and glorify human spirit by recognizing in **every walk of life,** those who achieved outstanding accomplishments or who made major contributions. This could include all sports, business, social service, engineering, science, acting, gardening, architecture, politics, civic contribution to make villages and towns clean and beautiful, military service, teaching, and house decorating, to name a few. Individuals will have that extra motivation to do their best when there exists the possibility of recognition at community, district, provincial and national levels.

People who are committed to work ethic and giving 100%+ to whatever they do are most apt to be accomplishment oriented. They have the desire and motivation to initiate and/or participate in community and other activities which contribute to enrichment of life.

Conclusions

In this chapter we discussed a set of social values which are very basic to developing attitudes necessary for successfully building a progressive, caring, cooperative, and civil society. The basic assumption underlying these is that the society wants to build a materially prosperous and fulfilling society. The emphasis is on developing practical and sensitive citizens who question everything, yet respect fellow human beings and the environment around them. When a society and its citizens have these attributes they are better prepared to build a strong economy based on sound social values.

These values will have to be explained and rationalised to the population within the context of other values if they are to gain acceptance. These new values must be consistent with other values including religious ones, otherwise people will find them difficult to accept. For example, it won't be easy for upper caste Hindus to accept equality of other human beings and thus they will have trouble to believe in the dignity of work. Adopting new values is always a slow and difficult process often accompanied with doubts and reservations. Some ideas will be presented later in the book on how this can be done.

Chapter 5

Political Values

These values help shape the political relationships among the citizens and their government, and the conduct of the government in international politics and relations. They also determine government's ability to govern.

As indicated earlier, Hindus lack the ability to govern for the simple reason that they lost practice of it while living under colonial rule for nearly one thousand years. It is not a reflection on their intellect because they have the capacity to relearn as fast as they want. They have demonstrated this in their adaptation and practice of democracy. Many consider Indian democracy as stable and vibrant. But in the actual governing of the country, lack of experience clearly shows. Politicians' understanding of economic development, trade, finance, international relations, national security and so on, is far from adequate. Subjects such as organisation and management have very little meaning to them; nor can they be trusted in the judicious use of power. All of these inadequacies have contributed to only modest gains in economic and social development, lapses in national security, and very little influence, if any, for India in international affairs.

Politicians fail to recognise that governing a country requires vision, conviction, focus, commitment, and most of all decisive action. They also do not possess the values necessary to guide them through tough and complex choices.

In this chapter a set of political values commonly found in developed and fast developing countries is presented which Hindu society will have to adopt if India is to develop into a respected economic and political power. They are:

1. Have a long term vision for the country and make fundamental decisions consistent with it.
2. Economy makes possible everything else.
3. Reliability and dependability of policies.
4. Less rhetoric and more action orientation.
5. Never back down from defending national objectives in international arena.
6. Always engage with major powers. Never shrink from competing with them in economics, trade, and on international issues
7. Always be prepared to fight to defend national interests, even if it means going to war.
8. Give material, moral, and military support to allies and friendly countries when they are in need.

The last five values are particularly applicable for those countries which aspire to become a major power.

Have Long-term Vision for the Country

Countries such as the United States have a vision as to the kind of country they want to be, and the leadership of the country communicates this to its citizens and obtains their consent and co-operation to work to make that vision a reality. For example the United States Government is committed to retaining its economic, political, and military leadership in the world and has the support of a majority of its citizens. This vision would be just an empty dream unless it is followed up with action plans and resource commitment. In the case of the United States the country has plans on how it would retain its leadership position and commits whatever resources are necessary to accomplish it. For example, whenever the United States Government sends its representatives to India to persuade it to sign Nuclear Non-Proliferation Treaty it is a part of its plan to ensure its leadership position in the world. Likewise, the United Kingdom is committed to maintaining for itself a major power status in Europe, if not the world, and it has the support of its people; and it commits the necessary resources to accomplish its vision. Take Japan for example. Its vision has been to remain as the leading exporter of high technology products and it also has the support of its people and commits whatever resources are necessary to make this a reality.

The principal advantage of having a vision, which has broad support, is that it provides a sense of purpose and rallies a majority of population around it and also releases their energies for making it a reality. In addition, it provides a criteria for establishing priorities and programmes, and a measuring stick for evaluating the progress in turning the vision into a reality. However, the vision must enjoy broad-based support, at least among major political parties representing a vast majority of the population. Otherwise it gets changed every time a new political party comes into power which only creates instability and chaos rather than any real benefits. To be useful, it should cover a time horizon of 20 to 25 years.

Another advantage of having a vision is that it provides stability for the business community to plan and implement major projects requiring large time horizons. Businessmen would be loath to invest, even in projects with a short planning horizon if they suspect that rules can be changed every time there is a change in government or a change in minister. Uncertainty and instability are deadly enemies of business. When a country has a vision with broad support among its population and reasonable assurance that it will not be changed for a well defined period of time, the business community will be able to plan and invest with confidence. China and South East Asian countries understood this well and therefore are striving to provide stability and continuity of their policies in order to attract investment.

It is doubtful whether the Hindu politicians have the discipline to truly commit to a vision; once a specific vision is agreed upon, it will require that everyone focus on work and work alone to turn it into a reality, leaving very little opportunity for rhetoric and second guessing. Many politicians will find it taxing and beyond their capability to work in such an intense environment. But the fact remains, countries with vision have been able to accomplish more than those without one. India's problems are immense and its poverty is unparalleled. They require commensurate effort and commitment which can be mustered only within the context of a vision. The present approach of rewriting rules and reviewing projects approved by the previous government every time a new government comes into power will take a very long time, if ever, to solve the fundamental problems of poverty. It is the poor who pay the price for this most destructive approach to building an economy.

When there is vision every citizen would know where the country is headed and this provides a reference point to evaluate whether proposed government policies and programmes are supportive and in conformity with the vision for the country. They also would be able to evaluate the adequacy of the programmes compared to the effort required for achieving the vision. At present, there is no simple basis other than ideological measures or some narrow yard-stick to evaluate the programmes. It should be pointed out that vision is not same as five year plans put out by the Planning Commission. The plans are for achieving a vision. An average citizen cannot understand the plans but he can understand and relate to a vision. There has never been a well-articulated vision for India since its independence. Of course politicians make vague promises that they will work to eliminate poverty, which are only slogans to get votes. Many of them simply do not know how to do it. No one knows for sure where the country is heading over the next, say, 20 years.

Here are a couple of vision statements for consideration. India will eliminate poverty and illiteracy by the year 2020 and **will do whatever may be necessary to achieve it.** The definition of elimination of poverty should be explained in some detail so that the public understands what that means. Or India **will become a major exporting nation of technology products ranking among the top three in Asia** by the year 2020. This is narrower than the first statement and also difficult for an average citizen to relate to it. The statement assumes enough wealth will be generated when the country becomes a leading exporter of technology products to be able to eliminate poverty which has proven to be the case in Japan. China, Taiwan and South Korea seems to be following this path, as well.

It is important to get major political parties to agree to a challenging vision statement for the country and get people to rally around it. This would require a firm commitment, pushing aside of ideologies and slogans, and communicating with masses to gain their support and co-operation. The present way of muddling through without knowing where the country is heading, in the long run, will only ensure that the fundamental problems facing the country remain unsolved. One of the serious consequences of this would be that the current economic and military gap between India and China will continue to widen.

Economy Makes Everything Possible

At the March 1998 gathering of the National Peoples' Congress in Beijing, the then Chinese premier Li Peng presented proposals to cut the number of state ministries from 40 to 29, eliminating four million jobs from the state bureaucracy. In the year 1997 when Hong Kong became part of China, the Chinese Government agreed to keep Hong Kong's economy separate from that of the rest of China. These two moves clearly show that the Chinese leadership understands the supremacy of economy over everything and that it provides the necessary wherewithal for the government and society to achieve all other objectives. Without a strong economy, society can achieve very little. This was the reason why they subjugated communist ideology to the requirements of the economy when they decided to fire four million civil servants. In the case of Hong Kong, they subjugated national unification and communist ideology to economic efficiency when they allowed Honk Kong to remain separate as an open society with an open economy.

In developed countries people believe the economy is the basis of everything within the society. It helps eliminate poverty, strengthens human dignity by providing the basic necessities of life, makes security and justice possible by providing funds to have sufficient police and well staffed judicial system, provides funds to care for the unfortunate and disabled, and numerous other things. Without a healthy economy none of these would be possible. One has only to look at Russia to see this in reality. Following the collapse of the former Soviet Union, the Russian economy collapsed and with it society itself collapsed. People do not have enough to eat, clothe themselves or keep warm in cold weather. Law and order has broken down and with it civility and hope have also disappeared.

The wise societies and their leaders know and understand the critical importance of a competitive economy for building a happy, compassionate, and fulfilling society. They do whatever it takes to keep their economies competitive and growing. China is a perfect example of this. They wisely chose pragmatism over ideology. They know that every slogan and ideology has a high cost associated with it and they only delay progress. What good are slogans and ideologies if they do not help progress a society as fast as and as well as it could?

Hindus and their leaders still do not have the full understanding of the important role that economy plays in nation building. This is partly due to lack of experience in governing, as discussed earlier. Equally important is that they seem indifferent and not offended by the grinding poverty in the country and do not consider the elimination of it to be their highest priority. They are not prepared to do whatever is necessary to achieve rapid economic growth in order to eliminate poverty within a reasonable period of time. For example, in early 1997 the Pay Commission report recommended to cut the number of civil servants by 30% over a period of ten years, which is a very modest target by any standard. Politicians however chose to ignore this and instead they agreed to give big pay increases to the civil servants amounting to about 1% of GDP. How does this compare to what China has been doing to strengthen its economy?

Take for example that for years now, India has been experiencing power shortages and outages, yet the government and politicians have been incapable of doing anything to resolve the capacity problems on an emergency basis. On the contrary, politicians throw road blocks in the way of major power projects such as the Enron project in the Maharastra province. Yet another example is that as soon as it appeared certain that the BJP and its allies were going to form the new government following the general elections in 1998, George Fernandes went all-out to scare the multinational companies away. Is that the highest priority of the country? Is Hindu society capable of eliminating poverty from its midst without massive foreign investment, when other developing societies, including China, decided they cannot do without it and are therefore doing everything possible to attract it? Can India afford the damage caused by these ill thought-out actions? Do the poor people in India really prefer ideology over having a descent standard of living without waiting forever for it? Until Hindus learn that a strong economy makes everything possible including elimination of poverty, and give the highest priority to eliminating poverty within a short period of time of say 15 years, they will continue to be nonchalant about developing the economy rapidly. Their fear of foreign investment and multinationals, mainly based on ideology, will certainly ensure that poverty remains well entrenched in their society for a long time into the future. India simply cannot get rid of its poverty without massive doses of foreign investment. Some industrialists such as Rahul Bajaj of Bajaj Auto Ltd. want the government to restrict the role of multinational corporations to certain sectors of the economy in order to balance the consumer interest and national interest. This is a slogan designed to hide the incompetence of some domestic companies. The sole purpose of business is to provide jobs and serve consumers with lowest prices. And there is absolutely no other purpose for business. It was established earlier that competition ensures creation of maximum number of jobs and lowest prices for consumers. If Rahul Bajaj's recommendations are implemented fewer jobs and higher prices will be the certain outcome in those industries which are protected from competition. All this is for allowing some incompetent businessmen to make money without facing the rigours of competition! Where is the national interest in all this? What is the basis for asking some businesses to operate in a competitive environment and some to operate in sheltered and protected environment ? Prior to economic reforms, there was hardly a product or technology developed in India measured up to international standards. Since the reforms, there has been a definite trend toward better quality products and technology. Why go back to inefficiency, poor quality and old technology now? How can the national security be enhanced by this? Hindus must resist these self-serving slogans of vested interest groups if they ever want to build a dynamic and prosperous economy. They must ask themselves why would anyone want to purposefully build a weak economy no matter what the excuse?

When every citizen understands that a strong economy makes everything possible and that competition is the true and lasting foundation on which it is built, then they will be in a better position to evaluate politicians, their slogans and policies. They will understand that slogans and ideologies have always high costs associated with them and that they are not designed to help the economy, and only a select few benefit from them.

It is well known that developed Western countries orchestrate their foreign and defence policies in order to help strengthen their economies. Hindus should learn from this if they really want to get ahead. The economy must become the centerpiece of everything.

Reliability and Stability of Policies

In a democracy, reliability and stability of policies is relative because change in governments usually results in a shift in direction which can require some changes to existing policies and/ or objectives. In almost all developed democratic countries such as the U.S.A, France, Italy, and the U.K there are fundamental philosophical differences among the major political parties which inevitably result in change in some major policies whenever a political party controlling the government is replaced by another.

But when a newly installed government changes policies of a previous government when there is no significant change in objectives and goals for the future, it creates instability, confusion and chaos. Such actions can only be termed mischievous and irresponsible, taken out of spite rather than to help the country. For example the review of Enron's Dhabol power project following the election of the Shiva Sena Government in Maharastra can only be termed as mischief because they discovered very little that was improper or illegal about it. What this did was to create fear and doubt in the international business community about the desirability of investing in India. All this happened at a time when India was becoming very popular with foreign investors. There are numerous examples like this in India, where rewriting the rules is a favourite past time of some politicians as soon as they get into government. Why do they commit such irresponsible acts?

Politicians who want to rewrite rules or review projects which have already been approved, usually do not have the capacity to come up with good ideas to build the future or have no ideas at all and to compensate for this they focus on the past and try to rewrite it. It is always more difficult and taxing to develop programmes to build the future than it is to look to the past and find something to criticise or second guess. What kind of good plans and ideas have the leaders of Shiva Sena come up with, to build a better future for Maharastra after they came into power? Similarly, as soon as he saw an opportunity to become a minister in the BJP government, George Fernandes began to threaten multinational corporations with this or that, but he has not yet put forth any specific ideas on how the country may be able to generate trillions of dollars of investment required to develop the economy and thus eliminate poverty within a reasonable period of time. Or doesn't he care about that? He has been saying that multinational corporations do not behave well and that they are not meeting their export targets etc. He has not presented any evidence to show that the behaviour of multinationals is any worse than that of domestic companies. Is it not proper for him to first find out how difficult it is for **any** company to meet planned sales or export targets before he begins to accuse foreign companies. All this irresponsible talk creates nothing but uncertainty and fear in the investors' mind which cannot be helpful for attracting foreign investment.

It is important for the business community to have some stability with laws and regulations governing them so that they may be able to make investments with confidence and reliability that the rules will not be changed in mid course which would have negative impact on the security and/or profitability of their investments. Otherwise they will be forced to cut back their investment plans which will have a detrimental effect on job creation which India can least afford.

There are other reasons, as well, why some politicians want to change rules and regulations governing the business community as soon as they get into power. For some, profit is still a dirty word because their thinking is still rooted in the Marxist doctrines. In their view, profits are an illegal confiscation of money belonging to workers and so they do not see anything wrong with the business community losing their investments as a result of change of rules in mid-course. Some do not see a role for private business in economic development as they want government ownership of everything. If these two groups cannot see that the communistic and socialistic approaches to building an economy have been completely rejected by Russia and even China, and that these countries are going as far as closing down or selling state owned enterprises in favour of private ownership, they are either ignorant or completely out of touch with reality.

Some politicians who promote the Swadeshi doctrine do anything and everything to upset and frustrate foreign corporations. For these politicians, doctrines are more important than the most efficient and fastest way to lift the country out of poverty. They are more committed to their doctrines than to doing whatever will help the country most. They will resort to tactics to destabilise and demoralise the business community, domestic or foreign, and their aim is to rewrite the laws every time they get into power in order to restrict or evict foreign companies, thus creating tremendous instability in the business and investment community. Let us analyse this doctrine.

The philosophy of the Swadeshi doctrine is that it is preferable and desirable to have most, if not all, products and services produced by Indian owned and managed companies only, and that foreign companies should not be allowed into the country. This is the strict version. The more commonly advocated version is that foreign companies should be kept out of certain sectors of the economy such as consumer goods and defence industries and so on. Of course they attach patriotism and morality to this position which stifles anyone challenging or wanting to objectively and dispassionately analyse it. Anyone with a little training in economic theory will tell us that protection breeds inefficiency, which in turn increases unit costs contributing to higher prices. Higher prices reduce demand which in turn reduces output of the industry resulting in loss of jobs. Therefore protection amounts to loss of jobs. This means that people who do not have jobs suffer most from the Swadeshi policy. Also, consumers suffer because of high prices. Prior to liberalisation of the Indian economy prices were higher and quality was poor in most cases. This, despite the fact there was competition among the domestic companies. After liberalisation foreign companies were allowed to compete and the obvious result of that has been that prices have weakened, quality has improved, and employment expanded in industries where stiff competition has been allowed. It is difficult to imagine how anyone can argue that it was bad for the Indian people!

Now let us look into the famous slogan that "India wants foreign companies to come in to invest in making computer chips but not in making potato chips." Why not both? What is the danger to India if foreign companies are allowed into the potato chip industry? It was established earlier that increased competition creates more jobs, reduces prices, increases consumption, and improves technology. Where is the danger? Someone might say foreign ownership threatens the economic security of India! But, how? India can and does have laws to guide the behaviour of the companies. How can foreign investment in making computer chips does not threaten national security but the investment in making potato chips does?

George Fernandes and some BJP thinkers advocate that India should not allow foreign companies into the consumer goods industries, but they never clearly state their reasons for it. Consumer goods industries directly impact on the standards of living of all citizens including the poor. The cheaper the consumer goods the more people can afford to buy them. More and more poor people could afford to buy their basic necessities. Also most consumer good industries employ low skilled and unskilled workers, which means more job opportunities for the poor and uneducated. As the demand for consumer food items increases, because of greater competition, there will be more demand for farm produce from food processing companies which, in turn, would help to increase farmers' income. **There is no other industry that will have a more direct bearing on the well-being of ordinary people than the consumer goods industry**. The greater the investment in this industry the faster the benefits will accrue to the middle class and the poor segments of society. Any restrictions on investments in this industry tantamount to depriving millions of people of their basic necessities. This is clearly a case of sacrificing the interests of the poor for the sake of ideology.

Most food processing factories are usually located in rural areas which means they would be of tremendous help for reducing chronic high unemployment usually associated with these areas. It is simply suicidal to restrict foreign investment in consumer goods industry. There are unlimited opportunities for both domestic and foreign companies in the industry because consumer goods market in India is vast and starving for huge investments. When people have jobs the security of the country is enhanced, not threatened. Why would foreign investment in consumer goods threaten the security but not if it is allowed in other sectors?

The only industry that one may be able to justify restricting foreign companies is the defence industry. One can argue that it is risky to rely on foreign companies to produce armaments for defence of the country. Here again any objective analysis does not justify it as India buys a lot of its important defence requirements from foreign countries. Is it not better then to have foreign companies produce those weapons in India, in partnership with Indian companies rather than buying them from companies located in foreign countries? Decisions are best made when emotions and slogans are taken out of them.

Swadeshi advocates imply that India needs multinational corporations only for their technology which is highly misleading. In fact the country needs them for their technology as well as for their investment. India simply does not have enough investment capital for its needs. For example, India has the technology to build roads, power plants, ports and so on but these projects require massive amounts of capital which the country simply does not have and therefore it needs to encourage foreign capital to come in, which it has been doing with modest success. Swadeshi advocates do not object to foreign investment in these infrastructure projects but they object to it in consumer goods industry. What harm can foreign investment possibly do to the potato chip industry or any other consumer product industry? There is no way India can eliminate poverty within a reasonable period of time, say 20 to 25 years, without the inflow of massive foreign investment coming into every sector of the economy. Swadeshi advocates are misleading the Indian public by implying that it is patriotic and moral to support their half baked doctrines. Any objective and detailed analysis will show that they are completely wrong and that it is more patriotic and morally correct to do whatever is necessary to fast eliminate poverty and hunger from the Indian society forever. If foreign investment can help do the job faster, why not have it?

It would serve the country better to help those industries that have the potential to become globally competitive, such as the computer software industry, than to engage in retrogressive doctrines such as Swadeshi which help only a few inefficient and incompetent businessmen.

Hindus must think through this subject of Swadeshi carefully, rid themselves of this last vestige of socialism and bring some stability to the business and financial markets. As indicated earlier, without stability and reliability of policies, foreign investment will not move into India in the massive quantities that it requires.

Less Rhetoric and More Action Orientation

It was discussed earlier that one of the attributes of Hindus is that they love rhetoric. They have a special fascination and affinity for it and feel most comfortable with it probably because it does not involve any action or responsibility.

A classical example of rhetoric was the Non-Aligned Movement originated by late Jawaharlal Nehru, President Tito of Yugoslavia, President Sukarno of Indonesia, and President Nasser of Egypt. The movement was full of rhetoric but not an ounce of action or responsibility. Nehru excelled in it because of his command of the English language and of course his Hindu background. He moralised every issue and lectured the leaders of the Western world. The four leaders had never once taken any significant action to back up their convictions and as a result no one took them seriously what they had to say. It is interesting to note that after Indonesia got rid of Sukarno, the country reduced its involvement with this group and thus began to make rapid economic progress. On the other hand India, Egypt, and Yugoslavia were left behind struggling.

Another example is the G-15 group of developing countries organised as a counter to the G-8 group of countries. Once again, rhetoric dominates over action and the group has accomplished very little thus far. They could if they cut down on the rhetoric and quietly build bridges to the G-8 group in a constructive business like manner and thus try to influence its policies.

Rhetoric without action is debilitating and it diminishes the individual and society. Many Indians wonder why the world respects and listens to China yet ignores India. The main reason for this is that Chinese leaders are quieter and more action-oriented and therefore the world listens to them and takes them seriously. If India is to regain the respect of the world, it should begin by distancing itself from those organisations whose main purpose is rhetoric and lecturing yet are not capable of achieving any concrete results. It should learn to refrain from rhetoric in matters where it cannot follow up with action. Silence is golden in such situations. Asian tigers [Thailand, Indonesia, South Korea, Singapore, Taiwan] are good examples of this. They usually stay away or maintain only minimum involvement with organisations that do not have resources to act and take on responsibility. After Sukarno's departure, one heard very little from Indonesia, instead they turned their focus to building their country.

Also, engaging in projects to prove "I can do it too" without any intention to take them to their logical conclusion is also rhetoric. India exploded a nuclear device in 1974 but failed to press ahead and produce the weapons immediately following the test; it test fired long range Agni missiles but stopped short of producing them for defence. [The BJP government reversed these decisions after May 1998 nuclear tests.] These rhetorical actions accomplished little; they did not scare the enemies or won applause in the international community. The only thing they attracted was scorn from both. These half measures showed that Hindus didn't know what they were doing. It would be similar to the Tata family producing an experimental car just to show to the world that they can do it but would have no plans to manufacture it. Actions like these diminish the country and often place it in jeopardy. For example, India's actions prompted and motivated Pakistan to develop nuclear weapons and missiles to ensure its security while Hindus were content with their half measures. No one can blame

Pakistan for not taking chances with its national security. It saw a threat to its security and acted on it immediately. The same thing cannot be said of Hindus. Their reaction to China's production of nuclear weapons and missiles has been irresponsible and rhetorical. Hindu leaders were afraid to tell the world that Chinese nuclear weapons and missiles threaten the security of India. Instead they engaged in " I can do it too" rhetoric which has done little to improve the actual military strength and preparedness of the country.

One of the attractions of rhetoric, as opposed to action, is that it allows moralisation of issues which Hindus love, because it gives them instant gratification and a sense of superiority. On the other hand, choice of action delays the gratification as it takes time for it to bear fruit, which may not turn out as hoped. Action also demands an enormous amount of energy, focus, and risk. For example, proceeding with the production of nuclear weapons and long range missiles immediately following the nuclear test in 1974 would have been a major undertaking fraught with international pressures and potential for some form of sanctions which frightened many Hindu politicians and people alike. So they resorted to rhetorical moves and thus obtained instant gratification in knowing they could develop these weapons whether or not they are available for use by the military. Meanwhile the country's security concerns remained unresolved.

Hindus should realise that they do not have a monopoly on morality. It is dependent on the degree of social, economic, and religious maturity of a society. Every society has its own set of morals and tries to live by them, as Hindus do by theirs. Any objective study would confirm that. Societies and people who are more action-oriented tend to be less rhetorical, moralising, and judgmental because they understand how the realities of life force a compromise with ideals and morals. In advanced societies it is a constant struggle to balance old morals with national security requirements, and new scientific discoveries in such areas as genetics, cosmic sciences, and medicine etc. They do not cling to the old morals just because they are old if realities of life and new discoveries do not support them. The society, therefore, modifies them and rejuvenates itself in this process.

As well, the advanced societies shy away from rhetoric and rhetorical actions and most of them genuinely believe in the saying that "actions speak louder than words." They may gloat after something really worthwhile is accomplished, but not before and even that, in most cases, is restrained.

If Hindus want their country to become a major power worthy of respect, it would serve them well to tone down on their rhetoric and become more pragmatic, practical and let the actions speak for themselves.

Never Back Down from Defending National Objectives in International Arena

The United States fought a major war with North Vietnam and lost. During the course of the war and after, the United States Government and its people developed a grudging respect for the Vietnamese leaders and its people. It stemmed from the fact that the Vietnamese fought the war with unwavering commitment, motivation and focus despite the odds overwhelmingly against them. During the war the country's leadership may have changed the tactics of fighting the war here and there, but they never changed their objective of evicting the U.S.A from Vietnam. Even during the most difficult times, the leadership did not give even the slightest indication that they might reconsider their major objective. This gave Vietnamese troops unshakable determination and morale to do whatever was necessary to win the war. They knew their leadership would never change its mind on its main objectives, come what may. The rest is history.

Iran has been fighting a major diplomatic war with the U.S.A since its Islamic revolution. It has made it clear to the American Government and its allies, that it does not need them or their support for it to achieve its objectives. Iran has been willing to pay the price and do it on its own terms. So far it is sticking to its terms and not bending to the U.S pressure.

There are many such examples throughout history; societies willing to do whatever may be necessary without compromise in order to achieve their fundamental goals and protect their honour, integrity, and security.

Hindus lack the experience of holding on to their ground when the odds are against them. Since its independence, India has fought wars with Pakistan and China. In the case of Pakistan, India won largely because of its size, but was pitifully weak against the other and hence lost. China had chosen not to completely humiliate India and therefore stopped the war on its own but only after occupying large tracts of Indian land. Since then India has done absolutely nothing concrete to narrow the military gap with China. On the contrary, its actions, or lack of them clearly indicate that it has acknowledged the military superiority of China and has resigned to it. However, most victors of wars are never satisfied until they have completely humiliated and destroyed whatever shred of self-respect was left in the defeated. Consistent with this, China continued its pressure on India by helping Pakistan develop nuclear weapons and missiles and commissioned the same in Tibet. What is the reaction of Hindus to all of this? Not so much as a word of protest or demand that China remove nuclear weapons and missiles from Tibet and stop its help to Pakistan develop nuclear weapons. On the contrary they have been promoting trade with China, have welcomed President Jiang Zemin to India and rolled out the red carpet while he continues to humiliate India in every way. I doubt if there is any society in the world which would behave the way Hindus have been while their country's security and honour has been systematically and methodically undermined.

Of course, some Hindus will point out that India now has the ability to develop nuclear weapons and long range missiles which signifies that it is narrowing the military gap with China, and that its refusal to sign the nuclear non-proliferation treaty is clear proof that it can hold its own ground. These are all rhetorical acts. Unless India actually produces nuclear weapons and deploys them with proper delivery systems, not much changed. The country's security has not improved one iota by the mere ability to make the weapons keeping in mind that the aggressor controls the timing of attack and the kind of weapons used in the early stages of the attack before India has a chance to respond.

With respect to the long range missiles, it is well known that India bowed to pressure from the United States and hence suspended further development on them since 1996. As a result it lost precious time. It would appear that the decision was reversed by the BJP government in 1998. One thing that Hindus must recognise, if they ever want India to gain respect, is that Americans, along with Europeans despise the weak, and respect and admire the strong. They may not say it, but that is what they believe in. In fact most people everywhere believe the same. What is there to admire in a weak person or a weak society? Everyone including Americans and Europeans respect a country that defies them when its national security and interests are at stake. This is the reason why they have more respect for Vietnam, Iran, China, France who defied the U.S at one time or other when their national security and interests were challenged. The U.S State Department officials must have laughed their head off at India for giving in to their pressure on such a vital issue. How can the U.S.A or for that matter any country have any respect for India and Hindus?

Since its independence, India has not performed a single act that deserves the respect and admiration of the world. It is not because Hindus are any less intelligent than others, but this is due to their lack of experience in governing a country and their apparent unwillingness to pay any price to defend their country and their freedoms. Naturally, many Hindus will vehemently deny this, but actions do speak louder than words. The Hindu society still has to develop the ability to pursue its vital national interests without fear and with a singular mind and focus.

The U.S.A, China and other powers cannot have a monopoly on nuclear weapons and missiles. Why shouldn't India have them, given its genuine security problems? Why did Hindus let the U.S.A and other powers have a say in their national security matters ? No one else does! For example, Pakistan, China, and Israel do not seek approval from the U.S.A in the matters of national security and in the kind of systems they should have to defend their countries.

India's ill thought-out actions facilitated other countries to get involved in its national security issues when it could not bring itself to go ahead with actual production of the nuclear weapons as soon as its testing of the nuclear device was completed in 1974. Their hesitation showed weakness within the Hindu character and lack of understanding of national security issues. So the U.S.A and other powers saw a window of opportunity to jump in quickly and tell India what to do and they immediately ceased it. Thus a domestic issue has become an international issue.

Hindus have yet to learn that they cannot trust any other country whatsoever, especially major powers with vested interest, when it comes to issues of national security. Unless they learn soon they can be certain their history of living under foreign rule will repeat itself. The U.S.A, China, France, Israel, Iran, Vietnam, Russia just to name a few, will never allow another country to interfere or offer unsolicited advice under any circumstances in matters of their national security. They would not hesitate for a moment to tell any country which tries to interfere to get lost.

When it comes to security and other vital issues of national importance a country cannot afford to back down under adversity and threats. When it steadfastly sticks to its position it will not only protect its freedom but will also develop character, self-respect, self-esteem, self-reliance and self-confidence of the society.

Compete with Major Powers in All Areas

For a country to develop economically, culturally, and politically it must compete with the best countries in the world in each one of these areas. It must engage, interact, and compete with them until it becomes a habit, otherwise it will stagnate as in the case of former communist countries. A major advantage of this is that it forces each and every competing country to recognise its own weaknesses and strengths by thoroughly understanding those of it competitors; and develop programmes to correct its weaknesses and further reinforce its strengths if it is to successfully compete. This is a never ending process which goes on and on among all the competing countries in trying to understand one another and thus adapt to one another. When this happens there is a consistent flow of ideas and values among them which benefits everyone involved. One classical example is the "just in time production" management techniques pioneered by Japanese and aggressively adopted by Americans and the rest of the world.

Societies progress when they are open to interact and compete with others. Those that do not, have little pressure and motivation to change and therefore become stagnant, fearful of other cultures and economies and ultimately degenerate and become weaker. This is what happened to former communist countries who closed their doors to the outside world; within less than 50 years the societies became weak and crumbled. On the other hand Japan, after the second world war, interacted and competed almost exclusively with the United States and Western Europe focusing on trade, technology, and defence and this helped it become one of the super economic powers. Although Japan did a little business with Asia its focus, from the beginning, was mainly to successfully compete with the United States. Succeed, it did.

Another example is China. After the second world war, it has always locked horns with the Unites States in one way or another. Prior to the cultural revolution it was contesting militarily and post revolution it has been in constant competition with the U.S.A in almost all areas: trade, defence, culture, sports, and international politics which has helped the country progress enormously in all these areas. Without competing with the best it could never have accomplished the progress it has. One can almost say it is preoccupied with the United States, and lately it includes Japan. It may fight against them most of the time but its main focus is always on them. It pays lip service and interacts a little with the developing world but its preoccupation is in engaging with the super economic and military powers of the world and rightly so because by competing with the best it has a better chance of becoming one.

If Hindus want India to become one of the best countries in the world they must fully open up their society for competition and place greater emphasis on interacting and competing with the developed world with respect to trade, culture, international politics, military, sports, and technology. Some Hindus find this objectionable as they do not trust the West and are afraid that it might colonise them again. They cannot be correct in this assessment because colonisation as in the past is passe in the West. Not only will their citizens not allow it, but the presence of the United Nations will also discourage any such adventures. However the West would try to continue to maintain its dominance in world affairs, particularly in trade, international security arrangements, the military, and technology. The only way for India to erode their dominance and protect itself from the ill effects of it, is to compete with them and become better at it. Withdrawing into a shell by closing its borders and having only minimal contact with the West would only make things worse because it will reduce competition and widen the gap between India and the West. The chances of narrowing the gap are much better if it competes with them. Japan, South Korea, China and South East Asian countries have clearly proven this. As said earlier, by competing it is possible to understand the strengths and weaknesses of the so called "enemy" and only by doing so is there a better chance of lessening its advantages. Ignorance accomplishes nothing.

This is also a reason why India should also open its doors to multinational corporations. They are the best instruments to quickly eliminate the technology gap with the developed countries. They also bring in capital and thus eliminate the need for India to borrow funds for that purpose. Of course the country will have to set some reasonable guidelines to control their conduct and also ensure that a level playing field exits between them and domestic companies, but it is foolish to shut them out or discourage them from coming in. In some quarters it is fancy to attack multinationals and question their benefits; only the losers do that. Smart societies learn to harness them for their benefit and not shut them out. Some Indian politicians argue that multinationals need India as badly as it needs them; the real truth is that India needs them more, since there are many countries in the world trying to attract these corporations to invest in their societies. They in turn can pass up any country, including India, without missing a beat.

If India is to transform quickly to be able to compete with developed nations, then it will need to fill the productivity gap as fast as possible. This can be best achieved by focusing on eliminating the technology gap, and the multinationals are in the best position to help India do it and do it fast since they usually have an edge in technology, management, and capital. This does not mean that it should ignore its domestic industry. Presence of multinationals in the economy usually sets a benchmark for technology and productivity to which domestic industry can aspire and government should therefore help it with an appropriate policy mix to catch up without propping up inefficient companies. A domestic industry capable of competing with any should be the ultimate goal. The presence of multinationals is needed to pressure the domestic industry to become globally competitive, otherwise it may never happen.

A country whose industry is globally competitive is also in a better position to become strong militarily. A military strength based on a technologically competitive domestic economy would be in a better position to provide national security, than a military based on armaments procured from abroad or produced at home with an inferior technology. China enjoys an edge over India in military strength not only because of its numerical superiority and well trained and motivated soldiers, but also because of its technological superiority. The only way India can ever achieve military superiority is by gaining a lead over China in technology.

Hindus have the intellect to do it. But do they have the determination?

In sports it is more evident than in economy that competition is the only way to superior performance. Unless an athlete or a player competes there is no way of knowing how good he or she really is.

Developed countries welcome competition in all aspects of life because they realise that that is what helped them to get where they are. They also realise that superiority in technology, combined with willingness to compete, will ensure their dominant position and therefore they invest quite heavily in applied research and development. These countries know that a globally competitive economy makes possible superior achievements in other areas. It provides resources for building military strength, doing well in sports, influencing international policies and so on.

If Hindus want to develop India into a strong economic and military power they can do so only by competing with major powers in all areas including economy, trade, military, sports, and international politics. The country would become stronger as it learns to compete better. But in order to compete successfully they should learn to tone down rhetoric and focus on action.

Be Prepared to go to War to Defend Vital Interests

There is a great deal of truth to the saying that "the best way to ensure peace is to be prepared to go to war." When a country is prepared to go to war to defend its vital interests, it sends a clear message to all potential aggressors that they would not have it easy and that there is a price to pay before embarking on any unwarranted adventures. That was precisely the principle behind detante during the cold war which meant that both the United States and the former Soviet Union were ready to go to war, likely nuclear, to defend their vital interests, and both sides clearly understood that. In any conflict between them, if one showed any hesitation the other took advantage of it but mostly neither was able to force its will on the other. Today the United States is capable and sometimes does impose its will on Russia since it is no longer prepared to fight and its weaknesses have been exposed.

Another example is that the United States tried to impose its will on Vietnam but failed because the Vietnamese were willing to fight and they fought valiantly to the bitter end.

When both sides of an international dispute are willing to fight to defend their vital interests, it usually means that neither one can impose its will on the other, thus the most likely solution to the dispute would be an honourable compromise which both parties can willingly accept. When one party is not willing or is not ready to go to war, the dispute is always settled in favour of the one that does. Chances of a fair settlement of dispute in such a situation would be very slim or even nil. For example, a fair settlement between Palestinians and Israelis is not possible unless and until the military strength of the Arab countries is more or less evenly matched with that of Israel. The foreign policy of the United States is aimed at making sure that this will never happen and therefore a fair settlement is not possible as long as this policy stays in tact.

These examples clearly show that the only thing that ensures fairness in a settlement of international disputes is the willingness and preparedness of both sides of the dispute to go to war if they have to. The grudging acknowledgment by each party in the dispute in their calculations that a war can be very costly and the outcome very uncertain is usually enough to force them to act fairly and seek a compromise honourable to both sides.

Morality has nothing to do with solving international disputes. As we discussed earlier each country has its own set of morals and every country believes that God is on their side. Self-interest and what is possible will continue to guide the behaviour of countries in their approach to solving the disputes. The rest is all propaganda and posturing. There is nothing wrong or immoral about it.

If India is to settle its border disputes with China in a manner fair to both sides there is no choice for India but to be prepared to fight China. The Chinese approach every negotiation from a position of strength and they try to wear down the opponent. Hindus are afraid of China and they probably should be because since the last border war the gap in military strength between the two countries has widened in favour of China. Not only it has shown little interest in settling the outstanding disputes but it has been also doing everything possible to systematically undermine the security of India by providing military hardware to Pakistan, and some insurgent groups in the north east provinces. It has helped Pakistan develop nuclear weapons and missiles. China can see that India has not been making any serious attempts to reduce the military gap between the two, except for a couple of rhetorical moves, and that Hindus are afraid to fight it to the point that they do not openly object to it deploying nuclear weapons in Tibet or attempt to raise the subject in relevant international forums. India went a couple of steps further in its policy of appeasement. As noted earlier, it welcomed the Chinese President to India with open arms and promoted trade relations with his country to the point that the Chinese do not hesitate to dump manufactured goods into the Indian market and thus try to put Indian companies out of business.

Any country finding itself in a similar position would refuse to have diplomatic relations with such a neighbour until there was a clear signal that it would stop undermining its security. But why would China do that when there is no pressure or demand from Hindus for it to cease its provocative acts ? One has to conclude that either Hindus do not appreciate or understand freedom and security, or that they lack the necessary skills to govern, or are simply afraid to fight a war against China to the point they can't even bring themselves to systematically begin working to improve their military capabilities against it.

China's attempts to destabilise India will intensify further, should India ever show signs of forging ahead of it either economically or politically or militarily. It's in its best interest to see that India remain the poor man of Asia as that will reinforce its supremacy in the continent. One of the reasons for its military attack on India in 1962 was that at that time it looked as though India's economy was moving ahead of that of China's and so it wanted to put a stop to it by forcing India to divert its resources away from economic development. It succeeded to a certain extent. India still has the potential to surpass China. Should India ever pursue such a course China would not hesitate attacking it again under one pretext or other. But it does not have to worry, so far Hindus seem to be co-operating by not seeking to overtake China.

It would serve Hindus well to realise that they are culturally isolated within the Asian continent, if not in the world, and most of the neighbouring countries neither comprehend nor feel comfortable with their values. They care very little for Hindus and their interest in India is purely commercial or for curiosity. There is hardly a country in the world which treats India as a reliable partner or neighbour for reciprocal security arrangements as most find Hindu thinking on these matters is incomprehensible and unrealistic. Also, their rhetoric chases people away.

Survival of a society, depends on its ability to adapt to internal as well as external environment which constantly change and most societies find it difficult to understand the latter and adjust to it. One can ignore the external environment at its own peril. This is what differentiates successful societies from those that fail. The successful ones spend enormous amounts of time and effort in understanding the external environment and threats in order to adjust and cope with them better. If the rest of the world believes in going to war, if necessary, to defend their vital interests and national security then that is what Hindus will have to adapt to if they expect to survive and be free for all times. There is no getting away from this, unless they do not mind being ruled by foreigners again in one form or other. Pakistanis understand national security well and are willing to fight to defend it, without any hesitation or reservations. They acquired nuclear weapons and missiles and have put Hindus on notice that they will not hesitate to use the nuclear weapons to defend themselves and their interests.

Give Material and Military Support to Friendly Countries

It is nice to see many Hindus fantasize about India becoming one of the super powers of the world, and it does have the potential to become one. But they rarely stop to think of what this entails. Some mistakenly equate a large population as the basis for it and others say that the country has demonstrated it has the technology and capability to produce nuclear weapons and long range missiles; so, therefore India is qualified to be a super power. It is important to remember that these accomplishments are only a demonstration of capability but have not made any difference in the actual military strength of the country. That is the reality!

If one carefully studies super powers on the Security Council of the United Nations, one will notice that not only do they have the technology to make sophisticated weapons but they also have weapons in quantities that allows them considerable **freedom of action** in international affairs which others do not have. They can impose their will, if they chose to, to influence the outcome of international issues. India does not have the military strength to assert for itself freedom of action in international affairs.

Another feature of these super powers is their willingness to fight when their security interests are at stake. India has not shown that it has the will or the capability to fight. Its wars with Pakistan are related to partition and based on religious hatred. So far it has shown no desire to fight China, if it has to, to defend its interests.

Yet another very important characteristic of these super powers is that they make friends and allies with countries they consider strategic, forge security arrangements with them, and offer material and military support to them as well. They will not hesitate to defend them whenever it is required.

More importantly the super powers take initiatives to change world order with the support of their friends and allies. They have the freedom of action derived from their military and economic power to try to shape the world in a way which ensures their leadership for as long as possible. They make no apologies for this and tell the world that it is their responsibility and right to do so.

India has no reliable friends and allies of any significance. Of course it has trading partners, but they should not be confused with allies and friends who depend on one another for security, military hardware, common defence arrangements and commitments, and co-ordinate their policies and approaches in international affairs. India does not have similar arrangements with any other countries other than Sikkim and Bhutan.

Hindus hesitate when it comes to fighting for their own security let alone others'. As discussed earlier, other countries find Hindu culture and values uncomfortable when it comes to such matters as defence, security, and world order because they tend to be out of touch with realities with their excessive moralisation and rhetoric when indeed action may be required. Simply put, other countries cannot rely on Hindus on these matters.

The first prerequisite for a country trying to become a power is to have considerable military strength, somewhat comparable to existing powers, permitting it some degree of **freedom of action** in international affairs enabling it to impose its views if and when it is in its interest to do so. It should be noted that there is a clear difference between capability and actual military strength. Japan and Germany have the capability to become super military powers. They have the technology and resources to be able to do it. Once they make a decision to become a military super power, it will take at least five to ten years to become one, if not longer. Until then very few countries will recognise them as super military powers. In the case of India, it will take much longer since its resources are limited, its technology base not yet comparable to international standards, and decision making is very slow even during the best of times. Without military strength and a strong economy supporting it there is no freedom of action and a country without it can never be a super power.

The second prerequisite is to offer and share military strength to guarantee the security of smaller countries in the area within the circle of its influence. If China, for instance, is seen as a threat to their security by smaller countries in South East Asia, India should be able to forge alliances with those countries and guarantee their security. It is an awesome responsibility. Are Hindus capable and reliable enough to take on such a responsibility? If the answer is yes then they should behave and make decisions accordingly.

Without reliable friends and allies no country can become a power! If Hindus want India to become a power they will have to institute policies and programmes to enable it to fulfill at least the first prerequisite first, that is acquire freedom of action in international affairs by building sufficient military strength.

The values presented in this chapter go against the grain of most Hindus and they will find it most difficult to comprehend and accept them. The society has had no experience in governing for about 1500 years. It is an awesome responsibility to govern a country like India under the best circumstances. Some of the values presented here demand a great deal of change in Hindu outlook and in their approach to govern. They have to establish themselves as practical, assertive, reliable and capable of doing whatever is required of them both in domestic and international politics. It is often said that politics is an art of compromise. If that is true, Hindus must recognise that the weak always wind up with a lot less than the strong at any bargaining table, especially in the international arena.

Political decisions should always be firmly grounded in reality. Every move away from it will be at a cost, sometimes a very high cost. One of the problems with rhetoric and moralising is that it moves one away from realism and commits one to ideologies and slogans which quite often have a high cost associated with them. The Western countries understand this only too well. They do not hesitate for a second to sacrifice, if necessary, whichever of their ideals may be contributing to moving them away from reality, especially when the stakes are high. This is exactly why the United States government supports dictatorial and communist regimes over democratic countries whenever its national interests dictate that it should, despite its professed ideal of defending freedom everywhere. It chooses China over India every time. It sided with Iraq in its border war with Iran, etc.

A society whose politics are solidly grounded in reality has a far better chance of succeeding in building a strong economy and also defend itself from threats to its security than the one that does not.

Chapter 6

National Security Values

National security is the task of ensuring that borders, freedoms, and other vital interests of a society are protected from unfriendly neighbouring countries, and colonial powers. The most important tools used for this purpose are the military force, security arrangements with other countries, and of course diplomacy; but most countries with serious security problems prefer to depend on their own military strength than seek help or protection from other countries.

Countries which are ruled by totalitarian governments or some form of dictatorship such as China, usually do not require nor ask their citizens to get involved in national security issues unless there is a major war threatening the very existence of the country. These governments usually have a powerful military to keep them in power as well as to take on the responsibility for national security.

However, in a democratic country citizens' involvement in national security matters is important and unavoidable, especially when there is a clear threat to the security of the country. It cannot cope effectively with outside threats without the participation and support of its citizens which in turn depends on their understanding and awareness of the issues. Patriotism of citizens also plays a vital role in national security. The greater the patriotism the greater the commitment of citizens to protect and defend the country.

A study of democratic countries which have successfully fought outside threats to their security would indicate the following elements in their values:

1. Citizens' commitment to national security.
2. Citizens' involvement in national defence preparedness.
3. Extreme sensitivity to actual as well as perceived threat to national security.
4. Do not let outsiders have any say in national security matters.
5. Weapon systems based on superior technology.
6. Weave a web of alliances to supplement military effort.

Each one of the above points will be analysed in the Indian context.

Citizens' Commitment to National Security

Allied forces were able to defeat Nazi Germany because of their citizens' involvement and commitment to national security. People understood how important it was to defeat Hitler. Vietnamese army was able to defeat France and the U.S.A because of their people's commitment and sacrifices. India was able to evict the British because of the same reasons. The U.S.A and the U.K always involve themselves in some war or other claiming that it was necessary to defend their national security. Without the understanding and commitment of their citizens it is simply not possible to engage in these adventures. In a democratic country, citizens understanding and commitment to national security issues is essential for it to be able to successfully cope with major challenges and threats to its security.

Indian society is a conglomeration of several different groups consisting of several religions and their sub groups such as castes, geographic groups [north versus south etc.], racial minorities [e.g. tribal groups in the north east], and language groups etc. Why should these vastly diverse groups love India and be motivated to ensure its security? It is doubtful anyone has an easy answer to this!

India is poor and has been working to improve the living standards of its people with reasonable success, but almost all Asian countries have been doing better than India in economic development over the past twenty years. In this respect some groups in India are unhappy with the rate of economic development in the country and large sections of the poor are also unhappy since they are benefiting very little from the development. Many groups also feel oppressed due to such factors as caste, religion, language and so on. Therefore, how can a society with so many divisions find something in common which can motivate them all to be highly committed to national security? What is that common asset of the country that all groups can easily relate to and be proud of and which they want to protect more than anything?

No other Asian country, with the exception of Japan, has as open and as dynamic a democracy as India. Even a well developed country like Singapore has only an orchestrated democracy because its leaders are afraid of a fully open democracy. Indians should be genuinely proud that they have unrestricted freedom of expression, worship, assembly, and an independent judiciary. Undoubtedly, there are some imperfections in it such as allowing criminals to contest in elections, and that some minority groups still feel threatened, but these will be corrected eventually. The point is that no other country in Asia has a better functioning democracy than India. Almost all Indians would agree that they should zealously guard and protect their freedoms and democracy and would be prepared to defend them at any cost. They should justifiably feel proud that they make democracy work while the rest of Asia can't.

The Indian government should actively promote programmes and measures to deepen the understanding and love of democracy of its people and encourage them to participate and strengthen it. It should set aside a day called, say, "democracy day" for Indians of all races, religions, castes, languages, and regions to come together to celebrate their common bond, democracy, and remind themselves that they are the only ones fortunate enough to enjoy unfettered democracy in the whole of Asia.

Unless Indians have something along the lines suggested above that they can recognise, experience, and feel proud of, they will have little reason to get excited about and committed to national defence and security. When people's beliefs are based on an understanding that they really have something worth protecting, then there is a better chance that they would develop a strong commitment and loyalty to defend it.

Also, societies which are progressive and prosperous are less prone to internal divisions and dissensions because they can create an environment in which different minority groups can work together and reach their potential. Citizens would be proud of such a society and would want to protect and defend it. Therefore economic and social progress is also vital to gaining citizens' commitment to national security.

In developed countries such as the U.S.A, Japan, Germany, and the U.K the citizens are very proud of their freedoms and their way of life and are prepared to do anything to protect them and their country. They are proud of the accomplishments of their societies and feel that they must protect the values which made those accomplishments possible. These strong feelings for their society and their country feed onto themselves as the society accomplishes more and more things which make its citizens proud. Conversely, if a country has only a few, if any significant accomplishments to its credit, it then becomes hard to hold the society together and get people to make sacrifices to protect it.

Therefore it is important that citizens feel they really have something worthwhile to protect if a country is to survive in the long run, especially a country as diverse as India. Otherwise it will fall apart like former Yugoslavia and Soviet Union.

Citizens' Involvement in National Defence Preparedness

It goes without saying that a nation is more secure when its citizens love their country, are prepared to defend it, and have some basic skills and training to do so. Until recently it was a requirement in the United States for all young men to enlist with the armed forces for a period of six months in order to receive military training when they reached 18 years of age. In addition they have other programmes such as reserve officers training corps for able bodied adults etc. In other countries such as Taiwan, Turkey, and Israel their youth are required to receive mandatory military training when they reach a certain age. Quite often they are sent into actual combat.

In some countries, not only the youth but also adults are required to receive basic military training on a part-time basis [e.g. a couple of times a week during evenings or weekends] with the expectation that they might be called to serve their country in emergency situations during a war.

There are two major advantages to having citizens receive military training. First, it enhances their patriotism and understanding of national security and defence. Second, it broadens the trained human resources pool from which the military can draw its additional requirements in emergency situations thus allowing it to have a smaller permanent military establishment in normal times. Also the trained adult citizens can support and supplement the military efforts, if required in activities such as an orderly evacuation or defence of villages or towns if enemy troops succeeded in forcing their way into the country and so on.

In India's case, its citizens for the most part are ill-equipped in their abilities to understand national security and defence matters, and they also lack training to be able to help the country in emergency situations. Many are patriotic and want to help the country but they lack training. They would know nothing on how to organize, for example, during a panic situation into groups and take charge in order to be able to tackle problems in an orderly manner. Some form of military training would correct many such problems. The training would also teach them discipline and an organised approach to problem solving which should be of great help in their daily lives as well.

When citizens have basic understanding of national security issues and have some military training the government would be more alert to national security threats and also be able to make decisions knowing that its citizens are well informed and capable of making significant contribution to military effort, if necessary.

As for the cost, India can afford if it begins the training programmes small scale and gradually expands them to include more and more adults. Initially, at least one training school per province organised to give four to six weeks of intensive training for at least a dozen able bodied adults from each and every village and proportionately larger numbers from towns and cities would be a good start. As resources permit they could expand to cover a good percentage of the population. In addition it should be made compulsory for young people to serve in the military for at least six months, similar to programmes in Turkey, Israel, etc. In order to keep costs under control, up to ten per cent of the current permanent military force may be replaced with young trainees on a rotation basis and gradually increase the percentage to a maximum, of say, thirty-five per cent. Military experts can probably suggest a better scheme than this, once the fundamental decision to give some form of military training to civilians is made by politicians.

In due course, as the pool of citizens with military training expands, society will have the knowledge to better understand national security and defence matters and be able to participate in the development of policies in these areas. At the present time these are the exclusive preserve of the elite with very little input from citizens. In addition, the tremendous positive impact these training programmes can also have on the character development of the nation cannot be over-estimated. This will probably wind up to be the greatest benefit of all, and Indian society will never be the same again. It will develop tremendous confidence in itself and will face national security issues in a realistic and responsible manner.

Extreme Sensitivity to Actual, as well as Perceived Threats to National Security

Countries such as the U.S.A, Turkey, Israel, Pakistan, and China act decisively to any actual or perceived threats to their national security. Most of them try to anticipate the likely sources of threat and take measures to neutralize them before they become a reality. When it comes to national security they do not trust anyone and do not take risk of getting caught off guard. One simple mistake can cause loss of freedom or territory for years.

The United States Government precipitated an international crisis when it found out that the former Soviet Union moved missiles into Cuba. Israel bombed and destroyed nuclear facilities under construction in Iraq before they became a real threat. Pakistan did not sit idly by when India exploded nuclear device in 1974. It has developed its own nuclear capabilities ever since. China helped North Korea and North Vietnam when they were fighting the United States in order to ensure that these countries are ruled by friendly governments and that the U.S military did not get close to its borders.

Obviously the principle behind these actions is that a country should deal with threats in the early stages, before it is too late or they become too big to handle or too costly to deal with in terms of man power and material requirements. Precious time can be lost if a country hesitates or waits to see if potential threats turn real. Sometimes the threatening country can back off when it notices that its intended target is taking effective counter-measures. Therefore, experienced countries are always alert and ready looking into their radar screen and searching for potential threats, before they become a reality.

Hindus' lack of experience to govern is evident. While China has been building massive military strength and also helping Pakistan develop nuclear weapons and missiles, Hindus have not been particularly disturbed by it. It is hard to imagine any country responding this way when faced with such major threats to its national security. Against whom do they think China has been building up its military might? The answer has to be either Russia, or Japan or India, or a combination there of. It does not need as big a military establishment to fight other neighbouring countries and also it has not shown any interest to engage in oversees [beyond Asia] military adventures.

Societies which value their freedoms, and integrity of their territory, take every threat seriously and try to deal with it the best way they can. They do not take any threat lightly. Hindus have yet to develop sensitivity, wisdom, and most of all courage to deal with threats to national security. They are particularly afraid of China and use rhetoric to hide their fear. Until George Fernandes articulated the Chinese threat soon after he became the Defence Minister in 1998, Hindus were living under the delusion that China was not a serious threat to their security. They forgot that the day before it attacked India in 1962, the then Chinese premier, Chou En lai, was telling the late Nehru and others who cared to listen, *Hindi Chini bhai bhai.* Hindus should never forget it. India should continue its good relations with China. But, at the same time, if India does not beef up its military strength, commensurate with the build up of China's it would be irresponsible, immature, and suicidal. How can China be offended if India strengthens its military capabilities while it is furiously doing the same itself? If

Hindus allow their fear of China to emasculate them from taking action to improve their defences, China would be the first to know it. This was the reason, it confidently went ahead and commissioned nuclear weapons and missiles in Tibet knowing Hindus will not dare to fight it. China was right. There was hardly any reaction from anyone in the government to these provocative acts until Mr. George Fernandes arrived on the scene as Defence Minister in 1998 and brought the whole matter to the attention of Indian public. Hindus should be aware that sensitivity to threats and perceived threats is the first step in national defence. If they miss the first step, it might be difficult, if not impossible, to catch up with what needs to be done in the remaining steps. It would be irresponsible on the part of Indian government if it does not go ahead and commission nuclear weapons and missiles along the Indo-Chinese border to offset Chinese nuclear weapons in Tibet.

In defence, preparation is everything because the aggressor controls the timing. This is a major reason why experienced countries remain alert at all times, especially when there are outstanding disputes with neighbours who are resourceful and ambitious.

Do not let Foreigners have a say in National Security Matters

National security is the critical aspect of nationhood. Each country's security needs are unique to its geography, history, internal stability, economic and military strength. It also depends on the state of relationships with the neighbouring countries and their history, political stability, economic and military strength, international ambitions, and so on. It is very difficult, if not impossible, for one country to fully understand and appreciate the security concerns of another country except at a superficial level and even more so if it has some vested interest. It will tend to interpret the concerns of others from the point of view of its own interests thus distorting the picture completely to suit its own needs.

A classic example is the Unites States' intervention in India's security concerns and needs. The United States for its own reasons, decided to support and strengthen China as the super power in Asia and expects the remaining Asian countries to buy this policy. It has been trying to convince them that China is not a threat to their security and that there is no need for them to develop some counterbalance to the Chinese power. This is the premise on which the United States Government bases its interpretation of India's security needs. The officials of the State Department have no clue of Indian history, the security concerns imposed by its geography, and the seriousness of the outstanding issues between it and Pakistan and China. They down-play these concerns to suit their sense of world order.

The U.S Government will not tolerate any of its enemies supplying arms to its neighbours, under any circumstances, threatening its security, however remote. The Cuban missile crisis was a clear example of this. And yet it has been minimizing the threat to India's security of China's military might and its role in helping Pakistan build nuclear weapons and missiles. The U.S tried to dissuade India from making any military preparation to neutralise China's power. What is absolutely mind boggling was that Hindus went along with it in deeds, if not in rhetoric, until recently. They took a couple of rhetorical actions to show to the world that they are not bending to the U.S.A and the West by exploding a nuclear device in 1974 and test firing some long range missiles, but they then backed down from producing and commissioning these weapons in defence. It now appears that these decisions were reversed following the nuclear tests in May 1998. But precious time was lost.

Hindus have very little strength of character when it comes to holding their ground in the face of powerful opponents such as China or the U.S.A. They should learn from countries like Iran, Pakistan, Israel, China, South Africa and France. Some of these countries are friends and allies, and some are enemies of the United States but all of them defied it in no uncertain terms when it came to deciding on their national security objectives and policies. Take for instance Pakistan which has enjoyed friendly relations with the United States ever since its creation and which has benefited considerably from the relationship. Both of them saw eye to eye on many international issues and co-operated fully with each other. But when it came to its own national security it had no difficulty in defying the U.S.A. Despite strong opposition and enormous pressure from the U.S Government, Pakistan went ahead and developed nuclear weapons and missiles. Muslim nations have always fully understood the meaning and critical importance of national security. On the other hand, Hindus still do not get it. Their lack of experience and wisdom in these matters, clearly shows.

Look at Israel. It went ahead against opposition from the U.S.A and world opinion and developed nuclear weapons and missiles in order to protect its national security. Similarly, China does what-ever it feels is best for its national security regardless of whether the U.S.A or any other country agrees with its decisions. Nelson Mandela told President Clinton, as clearly as he possibly could, that South Africa will continue its good relations with Cuba, Iran, and Iraq despite the U.S. Government's disapproval of it.

These countries know and understand the principles of governing; that their national security is not negotiable and that the U.S.A will never have their best interest in mind when it interferes in this vital subject. They can see that it is trying to serve its own vested interests. These countries will never compromise their security by listening to others because they know others cannot have the true understanding and passion for someone else's security.

Hindus lose their nerve every time they are confronted with tough choices. Until recently they have let others have veto power over their national security matters which was a clear indication of their lack of self-confidence and wisdom to be independent people. They have been afraid to pay the price whatever it might be to remain free for generations to come. This attitude may be changing following the nuclear tests in May 1998 but only time will tell whether it will last.

It is incredible that a country the size of India has, in matters of national security, succumbed for so long to the pressures of a distant foreign country which has its own vested interest and agenda.

Develop Weapon Systems Based on Superior Technology

It is obvious that when a country is confronted with a stronger opponent, there are only four ways to win; 1] to out-smart the opponent in strategy in the conduct of the war; 2] fight with weapons based on superior technology; 3] seek help from other countries; and 4] a combination thereof. The third option is fraught with danger because the countries which help will always try to extract a heavy price during or after the war.

India faces resourceful opponents in the likes of Pakistan and China. Pakistanis are proud, intelligent, risk-bearing, tenacious, and have a desperate desire and determination to outdo Hindus in everything. They believe that they are direct descendants of great Mogul rulers who conquered and ruled Hindus. Hence they feel they are better at planning and executing war campaigns and will never give up until they win like Muhammed Ghauri did. It would be a grave mistake for Hindus to underestimate Pakistanis. They have shown strength of character where it counted. They defied the United States and went ahead and developed nuclear weapons and missiles. They have shown their capacity to take risks by their intervention in Afghanistan and their tenacity by keeping the Kashmir issue boiling for nearly 50 years and are still unshaken in their commitment to Kashmir Muslims.

When it comes to China, India is facing a different class of opponent. China is ahead of India in both military and non-military technology, possesses nuclear weapons and missiles, and enjoys numerical superiority over India. It has solid experience in fighting wars. Chinese leadership has always displayed unwavering commitment to their fundamental objectives and their capacity for high risk, for example, in their disputes with Russians and Americans. They are tough negotiators and give very little, if any, in negotiations. If necessary, they will wait for years in order to get what they want. They are short on rhetoric and long on action.

The Chinese army is highly disciplined and motivated, well trained, has better weapons, and is confident of winning in any situation.

India must take into account the ongoing friendship and co-operation in defence related matters between Pakistan and China should an open military conflict take place between it and either one of the two opponents. There is bound to be co-operation and co-ordination between the two in order to increase pressure on India. One might say that India is cornered.

Given the above scenario, Hindus don't seem to have many options. The only sensible one is to develop and **deploy** technologically superior weapons, including nuclear weapons, than China has and at least enough to convince it that the risks are very high if it recklessly starts another border war with India.

In the case of China the main threat is along the border. It has the capacity to over-run the borders and pour thousands of soldiers into India by foot and by air. It does not have the capacity to mount a naval expedition against India. Therefore India must have enough power to contain them along the border. Nothing short of tactical nuclear weapons can stop them. Knowing that India has possession of such weapons which can be used in a limited way should be enough of a deterrent to China from initiating any border campaign. Only then will China ever come to a bargaining table seeking an equitable compromise on the issue of borders.

Pakistan can mount land, air, and sea battles against India depending on its battle plans. It has nuclear weapons and missiles operational but may chose not to use them unless it is cornered. Possession of these weapons by Pakistan will deter India from fighting an all-out war. In a limited war India cannot have much of an advantage because it gives Pakistan an opportunity to concentrate its military resources. Therefore the best strategy for India is to convince Pakistan that it will fight an all-out conventional war, if provoked. But it can do so only if India develops and deploys anti-missiles and sophisticated advanced warning systems which can help shoot down on-coming Pakistani missiles and aircraft, which more than likely will be carrying nuclear weapons, before they cross the border. Pakistan will try to use nuclear weapons on India if it looks like it cannot win the next war using conventional weapons. Pakistanis are desperate and want one more war to prove to themselves and to the world that they can win. Unless cool heads prevail, the next war will likely turn nuclear.

Any dispassionate and logical analysis would suggest India has no choice but to deploy tactical nuclear weapons and missiles capable of reaching targets in China and Pakistan. Also, it requires anti-missiles which can shoot down on-coming enemy missiles before they enter Indian territory. This is the only way to avoid nuclear wars with these countries and settle all-outstanding disputes on an equitable basis without anyone dictating or imposing the terms of settlement.

It is up to Hindus to decide whether they want a just settlement of the disputes with their neighbours or a settlement imposed on them. They should recognise that rhetorical acts do not buy peace, freedom, and security. Only the strong enjoys them.

Hindus should also realise that they don't have to apologise to anyone for choosing a nuclear option. All powers including the U.S.A, the U.K, France, Russia, China and Israel have chosen it. They have no more or no less moral right than India. In fact India is being forced to adopt the nuclear option because of the environment created by one of these powers, i.e. China. Hindus have the right, and an obligation to defend their country, freedom, and honour. No one can blame them, given the history of foreign conquests of their country. They just can't afford to take anymore risks with their freedom and territory.

Weave a Web of Security Alliances with Neighbouring Countries to Supplement Military Strength

During the cold war both the United States and the former Soviet Union had built as many security alliances as possible throughout the world in order to ensure that if there was a trouble in one part of the world they could count on stability and support in other parts to enable them to focus on the trouble spot. Israel made peace treaties with Egypt and Jordan and developed friendly relations with Turkey in order to minimize any threat from them while it is focusing on Palestinians, Syrians, and Iraqis. The United States made co-operative arrangements with Egypt, Syria, Saudi Arabia, and other small gulf states before it initiated the Gulf war against Iraq.

These countries recognise that it is to their advantage to have co-operative arrangements with countries nearby to a conflict or potentially conflict regions. Usually countries would agree to these arrangements if they can directly benefit in some way from such arrangements. For example, Egypt agreed to co-operate in the Gulf war when the U.S.A forgave a nearly ten billion dollar loan owed to it by Egypt. Similarly, Egypt agreed to a peace treaty with Israel when it returned the Sinai to Egypt and so on. When a country cannot offer some concrete benefit or other, very few countries would be interested in having co-operative arrangements with it.

China has been busy building co-operative relations in military matters with Pakistan and Iran, and also extending economic and political co-operation to Mynamar, Laos, Thailand, South Korea, and Vietnam. Basically China is isolating India in the region. Very few East Asian and South East Asian countries, if any, want to have close political or military ties with India. China seems to be gaining the support of Iran, as well. The contest is still open with the republics of the former Soviet Union and Mongolia.

Hindus lack the experience and skill required in negotiating treaties and pacts with other countries. In their 50 years of independence they have not been able to forge close ties with any country. This is partly because, as mentioned earlier, other countries find the values of Hindus and their rhetoric uncomfortable. More importantly, India being the poor man of Asia, does not have much of any thing to offer. No one would want to associate with the poor and the weak.

Basically, Hindus stand alone in the region. They are culturally, socially, and politically isolated; militarily weak and economically poor, but, by Asian standards, making only modest economic progress.

Hindus cannot hope to establish significant co-operative relationships with countries in the region until they become militarily and economically strong, tone down their rhetoric, and become pragmatic and practical. They must develop self-confidence and be willing to compete with anyone, not fear multinational corporations, and not let major powers such as the United States dictate what they can or cannot do. Then, neighbouring countries will begin to feel comfortable with Hindus and become more amenable to co-operative arrangements in security, economic, and political arenas. Until then India cannot have true national security.

The discussion in this chapter clearly shows that issues of national security are complex and tough and that they cannot be handled by the faint or the inexperienced. They require not only courage but also wisdom. Countries enjoy security only when they show an unwavering commitment to fight in order to defend their freedoms and borders, if they have to. Enemies can easily sense whether such a commitment exists, and if it doesn't they would not hesitate exploiting the opportunity. This is all the more reason why citizen participation in national defence is critical because it will give enough courage to politicians to make tough decisions knowing that citizens understand their decisions and will stand behind them. Also, when people are trained in basic defence skills they would be more courageous and willing to fight for their country if they have to, which would give the required strength to politicians to face up to tough choices in defending the country's interests. For example, the U.S. government always gauges the public opinion before it gets involved in any war, however small it might be. It knows that when people support the country's involvement in a military conflict they will be prepared to fight for it if they need to. That gives the government courage to make tough decisions when required.

China has installed various types of missiles and nuclear weapons in Tibet. India's response to this, until the Defence minister George Fernandes came along, has been to ignore it and to pretend that it was not a significant issue to worry about. It did not perceive any threat in these provocative actions. Obviously Hindus did not believe that these missiles and nuclear weapons were directed against India or perhaps they were simply overpowered with fear that they did not know how to react to. As mentioned earlier, any other country would have made it a major international issue, brought it to the attention of the international community, would have broken off diplomatic relations, and would have spared no effort in forcing China to remove them or would have installed similar missiles to neutralize those of the Chinese.

These Chinese actions weren't reported in the international press until the Indian nuclear tests in May 1998. And India had done very little to expose them, either. This was puzzling because many in the Western world did not understand why India was bent on developing nuclear and missile technology. Wasn't it the best opportunity for India to gain their understanding and support by highlighting the Chinese missiles and nuclear weapons in Tibet as soon as they were installed? There are only two plausible explanations for this. One is that Hindus were completely afraid of China and did not want to do anything that might anger it. The other is that they do not understand national security and not concerned much about their freedoms.

Hindus must recognise that they are making it more difficult for themselves by not properly responding to these clear threats from China. The best time to act is always in early stages. The longer they wait the worse position they will be in to defend their country or gain international support. It will never get easy. As mentioned earlier, India is cornered. It takes strong character and values to pull out of this mess that they created for themselves because of their fear to fight and lack of experience in governing.

Chapter 7

How to Fill the Gap in Values

The foregoing analysis identified a considerable gap between the actual Hindu values and those necessary for developing and securing India. Obviously Hindus want to develop their country as fast as they can and many of them would be willing to make necessary sacrifices to that end. But changing one's values and learning new ones under the best of circumstances is difficult because it is not only comfortable to hang on to the familiar, but also doubts will persist as to whether the new [to Hindus] values can really help as well as they seem to. The proposed values are neither new nor theoretical, they are practiced in almost all developed and fast developing countries. There can be no doubt about their ability to generate a high level of constructive energy in the individuals and the societies which adopt them. Evidence that they work can be found in India itself. Sikhs possess most of these values; they have strong work ethic, give 100%+ to whatever they do, have dignity of work, are full of self-confidence and have high self-esteem, are oriented to accomplishment, are practical, less rhetoric and more action-oriented. Is it any wonder then that Punjab is the most developed province in India and perhaps the cleanest as well? There are other groups as well such as Zorastrians, but Sikhs stand out as the largest group in India with the most appropriate values for developing and securing the country.

Also, it is important to reiterate that these so called new values are not religion based. They are secular and universally applicable. Their origin and the crystallisation of the concepts may be traced to the Western world but now they can be found in all kinds of cultures and the most familiar example of this to Hindus would be, as mentioned, the Sikh society. However there is one concept some Asians, including Hindus, may not feel comfortable with. The concept that all human beings are equal is somewhat alien to most Asian cultures, including the Hindu culture. The caste system gives rise to the belief that all human beings are **not** equal and most Hindus believe in this whether they openly admit or not. But it is interesting to note that when most Asians, including Hindus migrate to the Western countries they readily cling to and accept the concept that all human beings are equal, probably because it now suits their need to be treated as equal by the Westerners. And yet many of them continue to justify the practice of the caste system in India. It would not be easy to convince many upper caste Hindus of the validity of human equality concept. A majority of them will buy it but the real orthodox and fundamentalists will take a long time to come around. This problem is akin to racism in the Western world. Not all believe in eliminating it, but because a vast majority do, the racial minorities live in reasonable security and face only a few impediments in reaching their potential. The key to gaining support is education, persistence, and not to wait until everybody gets on the bandwagon. A lot of progress can be made with a majority support and approval.

Now to the most difficult of all the problems. **How can the new values be spread among such a vast number of people?** It was noted earlier that Hindus do not have community organisations of any sort which can reach people. Mainly, there are only two channels of communication available for reaching the masses. First, the educational system comprising all schools, colleges, and universities. Second, the mass media comprising press, radio, TV, and the cinema.

The educational system can and must play an important role in imparting appropriate values to the student population under its control. It has always played a role, either deliberately or by default. For example, the system has to bear most of the responsibility for why an overwhelming majority of Indian students do not ask questions or participate in discussions in classrooms. Similarly, it has failed to teach them careful observation and attention to detail of things and situations around them.

It is beyond the scope of this book to review the education system, but suffice to say it needs changing, if it is to play its due role in imparting proper values to all children, and young men and women who attend schools, colleges, and universities. It is well-known that the present method of teaching encourages intentionally or otherwise learning by rote, rather than by understanding. This will change only if the educators, politicians, business leaders and other distinguished citizens in the society get together and forge a national consensus on ways to improve the system, as well as devise a key role for it to play in imparting to students as many values as it is appropriate for an educational system to engage in. Certainly it cannot get involved in teaching religious and military values, but it can teach secular values which will make students better equipped individuals.

Educational institutions may be asked to add one or two courses to teach some of the values discussed earlier in this book beginning from first grade students in primary or elementary schools to university level students. The courses should be supplemented with opportunities for practising what they learn in the class room. For example it is all well and good to teach about giving 100%+ effort to whatever one does but it will have more meaning when students are assigned to projects which would allow them to put into practice what they have learned.

Also there are simple things that schools and universities can do to promote values, such as questioning everything and paying attention to detail. For example, make it a mandatory requirement that everyday, in every class, each and every student must ask the teacher at least two pertinent questions on the subject being taught. Students may be graded not only on their ability to give correct answers to a question, but also on their ability to ask proper questions to probe and understand a topic. A simple requirement like this could make a world of difference. It would not cost anything extra, however it would require extra time and effort on the part of students and teachers. But it would teach students to learn to question and probe for details in a very practical setting. At first the whole approach may seem ridiculous, but in time everyone will appreciate the benefits. The present passive method of learning would change to active learning.

If the entire educational system in the country takes on the responsibility of imparting some, or most, of the new set of values to all students who go through the system, the society will be transformed for the better in about 20 years. The country will experience a renaissance and revival unparalleled in its history. The society will be rejuvenated and would be capable of competing with the best in the world. A society that cannot or does not ask questions about itself cannot rejuvenate itself and adjust to changing times and demands. As a result it will be forever on defensive; looking to the past instead of looking to the future.

It would be more difficult to impart the new values to adults, and to those children and young people who do not go through the educational system. Here the mass media can play a very useful role. For example, a documentary film depicting a famous personality discussing the new value systems with real life examples of ordinary citizens who not only believe in but also practise in their daily life some of these values, such as work ethic, giving 100%+ effort to whatever they do, how they never stop asking questions before reaching a conclusion on an issue and so on, could be made and shown on TV so that millions can watch and learn, or at least become familiar with the values. Many people may already know or recognise many of these values in some form or other but may have never before heard them crystallised as values or expressed as aphorisms.

Another media approach might be to persuade cinema producers to make films with their story themes centered around a particular value or a set of values. A well made film can have a powerful impact on the minds of the audience.

The purpose of the media approach is to familiarise and convince the audience of the usefulness and the powerful impact the new values can have on an individual's life as well as on the well-being of the society. While the audience itself may or may not adopt the values in their daily lives they may, however, be able to impart them to their children or to someone they know.

The main difference between using the educational system versus the media approach is that education allows one to discuss and understand all pertinent details and also permits guidance and follow through at an individual level. The media approach does not, it provides no opportunity for discussion and clarification.

The subject of military training for adults and young people has been discussed elsewhere in the book, but it should be reiterated that it is critical to national security and character building and the Indian Government should give a serious consideration to the subject if it wishes to ensure the long term security of the country. The training will promote understanding and participation of citizens in national security issues which is essential in a democracy and also gives enough courage and strength to politicians to make correct decisions when confronted with tough enemies of the country. Given the long history of subjugation of Hindus, it is all the more important that ordinary citizens be involved in matters of national security in order to ensure that the governments are not taking unnecessary risks with their freedoms and with the territorial integrity of their country. Responsibility for security of the country should not be left entirely up to the elite, bureaucrats, and politicians.

This book has reviewed the values of Hindu society and their relevance to developing and securing India. It has shown the gap between their values and those of the countries which are economically and militarily strong. Hindus do not have a choice but to fill the gap if they wish to survive as a civilised society. The civilised societies do not tolerate poverty, filth, and erosion of human dignity and self-esteem among its citizens. They would act with a sense of urgency to eliminate poverty from their midst using whatever means may be necessary. These societies value their freedoms and their way of life and would do whatever necessary to defend them.

Hindus should realise that the world belongs to those who believe in it. Western countries dominate the world because they love life here on earth and are willing to do whatever is necessary to make it happy and enjoyable. They believe that the earth's resources are there for human beings to take control of and judiciously use them for their benefit. They sincerely believe in the adage **you get out of life what you put into it.** Westerners consider that life on earth is precious and are willing to put forth whatever effort is necessary to enrich it and make it more precious. That is the reason they adopt whatever values are appropriate to develop the world for their benefit.

If Hindus do not believe in working to make life on earth happy, enjoyable, and secure for themselves they will be dominated by those who do. Make no mistake, the strong and powerful dominate the poor and weak anytime and anywhere. This is an immutable truth of the Universe for all times and ages. There is no way out of this. The weak and the poor may moralise and philosophise all they wish, but that will change absolutely nothing. At best the rich may throw a few crumbs at them but they will never relax their control of the world in one form or other. The moral basis that they use to justify it is that the poor and the weak do not have the knowledge, experience, and wisdom to understand the world as well as they do and therefore it is their responsibility to be in charge and in control of the world. It is hard to objectively argue against it. **The rich and powerful willingly share control of the world in a significant**

way, with only other rich and powerful. Therefore, if Hindus want to be able to fully control their own destiny, and also share in the power to help shape the destiny of this world, they can do so only by becoming one among the rich and powerful. Their rhetoric and moralising will simply not impress anyone. Slogans and ideologies will not do either.

Becoming rich and powerful requires commitment, focus, hard work, and pragmatism. Slogans and rhetoric, for the most part, slow-down economic progress. For example, the latest slogan that "India should be built by Indians" probably gives a warm feeling to ideologists but it does nothing to expedite economic progress. It creates unnecessary fear in the minds of the investment community causing a slow-down in investment which in turn reduces employment growth. Is this what Hindus want? What exactly does the slogan mean? India is a sovereign country; Indian people elect the government which enacts all the laws of the land. If it decides that foreign investment and experts are needed and allows them in to quickly develop the country, does that mean that Indians are not building the country? Germany imported a large number of foreign workers right after the second world war to quickly build their country. Does that mean Germans did not build Germany? Intelligent societies use whatever means are required to quickly develop their countries. They do not imprison themselves with ideologies and meaningless slogans. Especially a country like India, with oppressive poverty everywhere, can least afford to say or do anything that would slow its economic growth. The only ideology and slogan it badly needs, is pragmatism and willingness to take whatever medicine will speed up its economic progress. Only those who do not care about the plight of the poor resort to ideologies and slogans which create road blocks in the way of rapid economic growth. We already discussed the fallacy of the slogan " India needs help in making computer chips not potato chips".

Ideologies and slogans are rhetoric and deprive an individual or a society of objectivity and rational analysis. They are least helpful for accomplishing anything on a large scale as they eliminate consideration and adaptation of certain valuable tools and policies. Irrational fear and prejudice dominate decision-making. Only an open mind coupled with pragmatism protects one from such a faulty analysis. As mentioned earlier, a recent decision by China to fire nearly four million civil servants is an example of triumph of pragmatism over ideology and slogans. The decision is in direct and open conflict with their communist ideologies and slogans. Common sense prevailed over fear and prejudice. The Chinese leadership has shown true courage and patriotism, and genuine love for their country. They embraced long term future of the country over short term peace with civil servants.

Hindus should recognise that the longer they take to eliminate poverty among their midst, the longer they will be under the control of the rich and powerful. They may delude themselves to believing that they can remain poor, secure and free from international powers by placing restrictions against foreign goods and foreigners entering into their country. An objective observation of the history of the world clearly proves otherwise. Closing the borders or restricting entry in one form or other to the outside world and trade, believing that it will improve national prosperity and security has been proven to be a fallacy by the fall of the communist countries, once and for all.

It would be tempting for some to believe that there is no need to adopt such values as work ethic but instead to let Indian people compete among themselves by restricting imports. India tried it under the guise of socialism for nearly forty years and yet it has not eliminated poverty. It also contributed to India falling behind other countries in Asia, especially China. Hindus should be aware that the greater the economic and military gap between it and China, the greater the risk to their security and freedom. It is not enough to make some economic progress, the gap with China must be narrowed if India is to remain secure. Relative growth is as important, if not more than absolute growth itself.

When an economy is opened to global competition the pressures of such competition forces the society to rapidly adjust and modify its values so that it can successfully compete. It will be forced into adopting almost all development values discussed in this book, such as work ethic, accomplishment orientation, etc. as quickly as possible. There will undoubtedly be some casualties initially but the society will eventually become strong and competitive in the global context. It is worth noting that every measure taken to protect the economy from competition will prolong the adjustment period, that is, it will extend the non-competitiveness of the economy for a longer time than is necessary. As indicated earlier, the unemployed and the poor suffer most from these policies. It would be better to pay some form of adjustment allowance for the employees of inefficient companies which are likely to fail when exposed to competition than to protect them from competition. The country would be better off strengthening companies which have a promising future, than protecting and subsidising inefficient and incompetent companies.

An open economy provides the best environment for learning development values. Society and individuals are best motivated to change and learn when faced with stiff competition. A competitive environment sets standards for every aspect of life, i.e. technology, research, medicine, sanitation and cleanliness, beauty, sports, communications, health, manufacturing, quality, productivity, education, skills, and so on. Without a standard it would be hard to know the level of effort required to successfully compete. Again, communist countries are a perfect example. They closed their doors to the outside world which resulted in absence of standards and competitive pressures which, in turn, led to degeneration of their societies. Hindus should resist the temptation of protectionism, however enticing it might be and open their economy to global competition which would be the surest and the fastest way for their society to learn and adopt the appropriate values to ensure its survival in the modern world. They must learn to trust themselves and be confident that they can rise to the challenge and successfully compete. Hindus certainly have the abilities to do it.

Hindus are out of their element when it comes to national security issues. Their inexperience in governance shows. They have not learned or changed much in this respect, even after living under foreign rule for a very long period. Their present-day values and attitudes towards national security are hardly different from those which existed in Hindu society prior to the foreign invasions of India. The internal divisions, unwillingness of people to fight, and reluctance to build military strength to match that of its neighbours and so on are the same today as they were in 900 A.D. The sad truth today is that they do not recognise the problem, let alone be willing to do something about it. Generally, societies develop and adapt appropriate value systems in response to security threats they face, but that is not the case with the Hindu society. The only responses the society shows are fear or indifference or wishful thinking, but beyond that it is not prepared to examine itself and bring about whatever changes are necessary in order to ensure that its history of foreign rule will never again be repeated. Perhaps this is due to the fact, as noted earlier, that there are no proper mechanisms available in Hindu society for initiating changes in their value systems primarily due to lack of organisation which can bring them together at community level. As a result, very little has changed in basic values and beliefs of the society. A small minority of well-informed citizens may have changed their values based on past experiences of the society, but their impact on society seems minimal.

The only mechanisms available to bring about changes in Hindu values, as noted earlier, are secular organisations such as educational institutions and governments. Luckily, the changes required are secular in nature and therefore these organisations can successfully teach new values if they are given an opportunity to do so. We have already discussed some of the programmes that they can offer, but these will take time to bear fruit. Security needs of the country cannot wait until then. Therefore the political leadership of the country will have to quickly change their values if meanwhile they want to successfully protect the security interests of the country.

In the short term, the two most important values that politicians will have to adapt are: not allowing foreign powers to dictate whether or not to induct nuclear and missile weapon systems and appropriate delivery systems into the Indian military, and a willingness to fight, if necessary, to defend the security of the country. Of course, politicians would deny that foreign powers have any kind of influence on security decisions, and would also insist that the country has always been willing to fight for its security; however, it is not the rhetoric but the actions that tell the truth. In their approach to the outstanding problems with China, the lack of these values is abundantly clear. The politicians were always afraid to clearly admit to the world why India needed nuclear weapons and missiles in the first place. India never needed these weapons to defend itself against Pakistan and this point was proven without a doubt in all three wars it fought against it. The one and only reason India needed them and still needs them was because China has them and this clearly gives it an edge over India; it has totally humiliated India in the border war between the two; and the outstanding border disputes between them have not yet been resolved. India was drawn into developing nuclear weapon technology in response to its defeat in the border war with China, certainly not in response to its successes in its wars with Pakistan. Hindu politicians were afraid to stress this openly to the world. Until recently, most of the world thought India wanted these weapons in order to defend itself against Pakistan, yet Hindu politicians did nothing to try and clear this misunderstanding, and Pakistan has been capitalising on this public relations blunder. Hindu politicians were afraid to stress the obvious truth that India needed these weapons to defend itself against China and that it would not require them if China were to destroy all the nuclear weapons and missiles in its possession. Why didn't they say it openly again and again, until the world understood the real reasons? The answer is the fear of China. Following India's nuclear test in 1972, if Indian politicians had explained to the world that India reserves the right to have nuclear weapons if China acquired such weapons, it might have put tremendous pressure on China to review its nuclear policy and also to come to an honourable compromise in its border disputes with India. Also, the world leaders might have been more cautious and less forthcoming in allowing China into the "nuclear club". Because Hindu politicians are afraid to openly object to China having nuclear arsenal, India's justification to have nuclear weapons was always based on false pretenses and eventually deteriorated into a contest between India and Pakistan. Even after the nuclear tests in May 1998 Hindu politicians were still afraid to openly tell the truth to the world that India does not feel secure as long as China has nuclear weapons and that India is obliged to have the same weapons as long as China has them. Is it any wonder then that the world community neither trusts nor understands India's intentions when it comes to nuclear weapons? Hindu politicians should realise that it is not in the best interest of India to hide the truth.

Instead, the politicians chose, in typical Hindu fashion, a rhetorical approach to the nuclear weapons problem which was to demand that all the nuclear powers destroy their weapons. In reality the nuclear weapons of the U.S.A, Russia, and France are not an immediate threat to India but China's weapons have been and still are. Rather than focusing on the specific problem with China, Hindu politicians decided to tackle a much larger issue of asking all nuclear powers to destroy their weapons. As can be expected, they have received very little sympathy and support for their position from the world community. India simply does not have the power and prestige to win on an issue of that magnitude. If they had just focused on the specific problem facing India, rather than on the larger issue, they would probably have succeeded in dividing and isolating China from the rest of the nuclear powers. Even some nuclear powers may have sided with India. But now India is isolated and treated as irresponsible and dangerous while China is considered reasonable and respectable. Since India has not openly finger-pointed China as the sole reason for its need to have nuclear weapons and missiles, the world continues to believe that it wants them to fight Pakistan, and as such is absolutely mystified as to why India would need them to defend itself from a smaller neighbour.

At the moment, there is absolutely no pressure on China either from India or from world powers to reduce or eliminate its nuclear arsenal or to settle its outstanding disputes with India in a fair and honourable manner. Why would any world power want to get involved if India itself does not care enough to raise the issue in international forums?

Why do Hindus behave this way? It can only be attributed to their fear of offending China and they are probably utterly scared at the prospect of being drawn into an armed conflict with it again. Absolutely nothing else can explain this bizarre behaviour. When an individual or a society is consumed with fear its behaviour turns irrational and counter productive. There are no easy answers for getting rid of Hindus fear of fighting China, if they have to, other than by initiating the build up of India's military strength methodically and quickly, with the firm objective of filling the military gap between it and China. This would be possible only if the economic gap between the two is narrowed concurrently, and all able bodied citizens of the country are given some form of military training. Only preparation reduces or eliminates fear. Ignoring the problem or pretending that it does not exist usually compounds it.

One cannot over emphasize the importance for India to have some form of military training for its citizens. Without it, the citizens will never have the appreciation for national security or for the importance of willingness to fight, if they have to, a powerful opponent like China in securing the country. Until then the country would be in no better position to defend itself than it was prior to the Mogul invasion. Hindus should be open-minded enough to learn from their past. Current national security problems dangerously resemble those which existed in Hindu India prior to the Mogul invasion.

Countries do not become rich and powerful, or poor and weak, by accident. The values of the society mostly determine this. The choices they make, the motivation, and the degree of effort they put forth to better themselves are all a function of values. Luck and fate have very little to do with it. If a society is to progress it should be flexible enough to examine itself and its values and modify them to rejuvenate itself to better adjust to the changing conditions and demands of the world. Hanging on to past values which have contributed, at least partly if not mostly, to the current unsatisfactory conditions within the society is not worthy of a great civilisation or a great society. It indicates an inability to change rather than anything good or desirable about those values. There are so many societies in the world falling by the wayside because they dearly hang on to their past values, some of which are no longer relevant and find themselves incapable of rejuvenating and adjusting to the new realities of the world. It is very unfortunate and sad to see them suffer. But the simple truth is: **what works well is**

worth hanging onto, and that which does not is not worth hanging onto unless it can be modified. This smacks of materialistic or utilitarian philosophy. But regardless of what it is, that is what is followed by successful societies all over the world, and it is they who are controlling and shaping the future of the world. And the cruel fact is that either one gets on the bandwagon or gets left behind. Those who refuse to change are indeed left behind and they have very little say, if any, either to shape the destiny of their own society or that of the world. Until a society becomes a member of the successful societies it does not have the clout or the resources to demand an effective role in controlling and shaping the future of the world. That is the reality. Countries such as China and Russia have accepted it for what it is and have decided to join the bandwagon. They obviously decided that it is not worth wasting time fighting a philosophy which works, at least for now. Instead they accepted the free market philosophy and most of the values which come with it. Some bureaucrats and politicians in India are willing to go only half way with free market reforms and its associated values which means they want to take twice as long as necessary to achieve the same results as China has. This is like giving less than the best effort one can give to do a job properly. It is up to the majority of citizens to decide whether that is a wise choice and what is to be gained by prolonging the suffering of the poor and unemployed, not to mention the high prices consumers will have to pay for twice as long as necessary.

Hindus should work to strengthen individuals as a means to strengthen the society. Their interests have received a low priority for too long despite the lip service politicians give to helping individuals develop their potential. Hindus must recognise the dangers of allowing the Central Government to continue to have excessive power at the expense of citizens' rights and freedoms. A society cannot achieve its full potential by keeping its citizens weak, illiterate, and unskilled. The government should divest its ownership in public sector undertakings [PSU's] and use the funds from their sale to develop infrastructure and to build vocational and trade schools in all large villages, towns, and cities across the country so that poor can have easy access to learn skills and trades they need to get jobs. In a free economy, every rupee tied up in PSUs is a rupee stolen from the poor. Now that the economic reforms are in place, there is absolutely no reason, other than ideology, for the government to continue to maintain its investments in PSUs.

Hindus have the native intelligence and are capable of doing anything as well as anyone can. But they have to become more practical and adopt suitable values for development, if they really want to get rid of poverty from their midst, which is strangling their society, as fast as any country has ever done and be able to join the ranks of developed societies in helping to shape the future of the world consistent with their values, beliefs and security of their country.

Index